Kids Around the World Cook!

The Best Foods and Recipes from Many Lands

Arlette N. Braman

illustrated by Jo-Ellen Bosson

John Wiley & Sons, Inc.

New York ▪ Chichester ▪ Weinheim ▪ Brisbane ▪ Singapore ▪ Toronto

Published by John Wiley & Sons, Inc.
Published simultaneously in Canada

Design and production by Navta Associates, Inc.

The publisher and the author have made every reasonable effort to ensure that the experiments and activities in this book are safe when conducted as instructed but assume no responsibility for any damage caused or sustained while performing the experiments or activities in the book. Parents, guardians, and/or teachers should supervise young readers who undertake the experiments and activities in this book.

Library of Congress Cataloging-in-Publication Data
Braman, Arlette N.
    Kids around the world cook! : the best foods and recipes from many lands / Arlette N. Braman.
      p.   cm.
    Summary: Presents information on and recipes for a variety of foods from many countries, including Sweet Lassi from India, Challah from Israel, Strawberry Soup from Poland, Kushiyaki from Japan, and Prairie Berry Cake from Canada.
     ISBN 0-471-35251-9
     1. Cookery, International—Juvenile literature.   [1. Cookery, International.]   I. Title.
TX725.A1 B73   2000
641.59—dc21   99-046110

Printed in the United States of America

10 9 8 7 6 5 4 3 2

For my dad, Michael Naspinski, who taught me about cooking
by adding "a little of this and a little of that," and for my mom, Josephine,
who introduced me to a whole new world of cultural tastes

Contents

Acknowledgments

I would like to thank Mrs. Bozena of Hamilton Elementary School in Stroudsburg, Pa., for "lending" me her fourth-grade class to test the recipes in this book. All of the kids did a great job! Also, a very big thanks to Elizabeth Decker, Nancy Spurkeland, and Callan and Abigail Braman for their help in testing and tasting recipes.

I owe a special thanks to the following people who shared recipes* with me: Milayna Goruick of Saskatchewan, Canada, for prairie berry cake; Naji Jabbour of the Ali BaBa Restaurant in Tannersville, Pa., for Lebanese baba ghanouj; Marta Hardy of Florida, for Cuban black bean soup; Engela Kemp of South Africa, for *potjiekos;* Laila Moustafa of Pennsylvania, for Egyptian baklawa; Josephine Lagos Naspinski of Florida, for Spanish saffron meatballs; Mary Nicholas of Greek Delights in Stroudsburg, Pa., for Greek hummus; Boonchad Pruettipun of Saen Thai Restaurant in East Stroudsburg, Pa., for Thai sweet rice with coconut custard; William J. Serow of Florida State University in Tallahassee, Fla., for macaroni and cheese; Grace C. Fener Markofsky of New York, for Jewish challah; Margaret O'Hanlon of California, for afternoon tea; and Joyce Wetlesen of Pennsylvania, for Norwegian nutmeg cookies.

All of the following people deserve many thanks for sharing information about favorite family dishes, lending me books, answering my obscure questions, helping me with pronunciations, sending out family email information requests, searching the web, and many other things: Dr. Ian H. Ackroyd-Kelly of East Stroudsburg University,

---

*In almost all cases, I made some changes to the original recipes I received from the people mentioned here. For the most part, this was done to make the recipes easier for kids to prepare.

for his expertise on Maori culture; Carmen and Jim Beaton; Denise Buoye; Rabbi Davis of Temple Israel in Stroudsburg, Pa.; Duke at the agricultural department in Alberta, Canada; Jean Field; Neil and Barbara Goldman for their information on Jewish customs; Sue Grillo; Marjorie Henry; Michael Hintlian, for his knowledge of Armenian foods and customs; Gwen Holmes; the people at India Gate Restaurant; Kraft Foods, Inc.; Michelle Lagos; the Monroe County Public Library, for giving me extended loan privileges; Kathleen Murphy; Brody Nancarrow and his "mum," Judy, and Leigh Dorey, for their information about Australian barbecue; Avis Neary; Lincoln Nkompela and Lorraine Jantjies of the South African Harvest Team '98 for their information about *potjiekos;* Jane Pace; Curt Paine; Carroll Pellegrinelli, baking guide at About.com; Pat Pinciotti; Nancy Robertson, for her fondue pot; Linda Schott of Sweet Creams Café in Stroudsburg, Pa., for making the New York egg cream we needed to photograph; Lucy Ito's Restaurant in Florida for setting up the Mongolian barbecue we needed to photograph; San Giorgio Company; Kazu Seto; Heide and Emil Signes; Richard and Maribel Signes; Gary Teale, for his information about Maori foods; Peggy Trowbridge, home cooking guide, About.com; the people at Uskudar Turkish Restaurant, New York City; Dr. Ralph M. Vitello, Dr. R. Squier Ball, and Liz Ruckel of the Foreign Language Department at East Stroudsburg University; and Jim Wallace.

Special thanks to Professor Russell A. Clark of East Stroudsburg University, for his food expertise and his willingness to help; and a huge thanks to Larry Kelly, *the* search engine genius of the web.

Many thanks to my husband, Gary, for shooting most of the photos for the book, for enduring weeks of taste-testing the same dish over and over, and for keeping the house functioning. Last but not least, I appreciate all the help from my editor, Kate Bradford, and from Diana Madrigal, Sibylle Kazeroid, Jude Patterson, and all the people at Wiley who worked on this book.

A Message to Kids of All Cultures

Cooking has been a part of my life for as long as I can remember. My dad was a cook in the Navy, and one of his first jobs was selling homemade sandwiches and coffee from a food cart. He loved to cook and always made it look so easy. I learned a great deal from him and would follow him around the kitchen taking notes. My mom was the baker. She created cakes and cookies with ease. I owe my sweet tooth to her. My grandfather worked for a caterer in Boston and my grandmother, who lived with us, taught my dad about Spanish cooking.

The majority of the cooking done in our house was not traditional American fare. My own roots are Polish, French, and Spanish. My parents filled holidays, special occasions, Sunday dinners, and almost any time with wonderful foods from many countries. To this day, I love cooking ethnic meals and eating out at ethnic restaurants.

The information and recipes in this book will give you a "tour" of countries from around the globe and a taste of foods from many cultures. I hope that cooking and enjoying these foods will help give you an appreciation of the cultures they come from. We all have wonderful things to share with one another.

Kitchen Safety

The kitchen can be a dangerous part of your home. Sharp knives, boiling water, and hot oil are just a few things that can hurt you. But you can make your kitchen safe by following a few basic safety rules.

1 Always check with an adult before cooking. Talk about what you are allowed to do by yourself and when you need an adult's help.

2 Keep the Kitchen Clean

- Wash your hands thoroughly before and after cooking. Also, always wash your hands after handling raw eggs or meat.

- Carefully wash and dry any cutting boards, countertops, or utensils that you have used for cutting raw meat before using them for anything else.

- Wash all fruits and vegetables thoroughly before cooking with them.

3 When Using the Stove and Oven

- Ask permission before using a stove or oven.

- Never fry with oil at a high temperature.

- When using a frying pan that contains oil, never leave or turn your back on the stove.

- Clothing can catch on fire, so don't wear baggy shirts or sweaters when cooking. If you have long hair, tie it back with barrettes or wear a ponytail.

- Spray a pan with vegetable oil cooking spray only over the sink—not over the stove.

- Don't overfill pans with boiling or simmering liquids.

- Never use the oven, handle anything hot, or hold a pot handle without a pot holder or oven mitt. Use only dry pot holders, since wet pot holders will transfer the heat from the hot item directly to your skin.

In case of a stove fire, have an adult smother it by covering the fire with the pan lid or pouring baking soda on it. Water should never be used on this type of fire—it only makes the fire worse.

Open pan lids away from you to let steam escape safely.

Always turn pan handles toward the back of the stove. If they stick out, you can bump them and burn yourself or splatter hot food.

Use long-handled spoons when stirring.

Never have little children in the kitchen when you are cooking. And keep pets away as well. Your attention should be focused on your cooking.

4 When Using Any Appliance

Ask permission before using any appliance and make sure you know how to use it.

Frayed electrical cords or damaged plugs and outlets can be dangerous. Tell an adult.

Operate appliances away from the sink or any standing water.

5 When Using a Microwave Oven

Use only proper, microwave-safe cookware, paper towels, paper plates, or paper cups.

Always leave a small opening in a covered dish so that steam can escape during cooking.

Never remove anything from a microwave without pot holders or oven mitts.

Always open the food container slowly and away from your face and hands so you won't get burned from the steam.

Certain foods, such as potatoes and hot dogs, need to be pricked with a fork before you cook them in the microwave. Otherwise they might burst.

Never cook a whole egg in the microwave—it will burst!

6 When Using a Knife

Always ask permission before using any knife.

Don't be distracted when using a knife—you could cut yourself.

Always pick up a knife by its handle.

For slicing, slide the knife over the food using a back-and-forth motion.

Always cut away from your body and away from anyone around you.

If the knife falls to the floor, don't try to catch it.

Keep all knives toward the center of your work space—never at the edge of the work space. Someone could get hurt.

Knives should be used only for cutting foods, not for anything else—ever.

Never put a knife into a sink full of water. Wash it immediately with a sponge, keeping the blade facing away from you.

7 When Measuring

Always put the measuring cup on a flat surface when pouring foods or liquids into it. Don't hold the cup in one hand while trying to pour with the other hand.

When pouring dry food, such as flour or sugar, into the measuring cup, lightly tap the bottom of the cup on your work surface to settle, or pack the food tightly, in the cup. Then readjust the amount if necessary.

Never fill a measuring cup while holding it over a bowl filled with other ingredients. If you pour too much and it spills into the bowl, your ingredients will not be accurate.

Measure salt accurately. You can easily add more salt to the dish while you're eating, but it is impossible to remove salt once you've added too much.

A Note About the Ingredients

You will be able to find most of the ingredients used in these recipes in your local supermarket. Some of the ethnic ingredients can be found in ethnic or specialty shops. For example, the rose water used in the sweet *lassi* recipe can be found in Asian markets or health food stores. I will always tell you in the recipe where an ethnic ingredient can be found.

If for some reason you can't find an ingredient locally, you can find it on the World Wide Web. But you must check with an adult first, because the adult will have to order it for you. Here is a web site address that is helpful:

www.askjeeves.com

When you get to the web site, just ask a question like, "Where can I buy German foods?" and you will be given a list of places to order the food you need.

PART ONE

Wet Your Whistle

If you're tired of the same old milk and cookies after school, why not have a spot of British afternoon tea with some biscuits? Or, instead of having a cold soda on a hot summer's day, how about trying a delicious glass of cold yak's milk, like the kids in Mongolia drink?

In Korea, kids enjoy rice juice made from rice, flour, water, and sugar. If you visit India, you might want to try *chai* (pronounced chi), a spiced milk tea that tastes like liquid pumpkin pie. Coconut and pineapple juice drinks will satisfy your thirst in Venezuela, where these and many other tropical fruits grow. Long ago, American Indians from many tribes made a nut milk by boiling chestnuts and hickory nuts.

The recipes in this section will give you a taste of beverages from around the world.

Afternoon Tea

Tea drinking had its beginnings almost 5,000 years ago in ancient China. One story says that Emperor Shen Nong discovered tea when leaves from the tea tree blew into water he was boiling. Curious about the scented, amber-colored water, he took one sip and the rest is history. From China, explorers brought tea seeds back to many other countries, and soon the whole world could grow and enjoy this new beverage.

Today, people drink many different types of tea, including Japanese green tea, which has a lot of nutrients and minerals; Ceylon tea from Sri Lanka (an island in the Indian Ocean), which has a sweet taste; and chamomile tea, a mild herbal tea made from chamomile flowers.

Many cultures don't just drink tea, they make it into a ritual. In Japan, people have elaborate tea ceremonies in which how you make the tea, how you serve it, even where you drink it are all important parts. In Turkey, the ritual includes taking a tea break during the work day and drinking the dark red tea in clear glasses.

England also enjoys its tea-drinking ritual. The habit of having an afternoon cup of tea and a snack between lunch and a late dinner began in about 1840 and continues today. People munch on tea biscuits, **crumpets** (small, flat, muffin-like cakes), scones and jam, or tea sandwiches while sipping hot tea served with sugar and milk.

COOKING UP SOME HISTORY

People drank iced tea for the first time in 1904 at the Louisiana Purchase Exposition in St. Louis, Mo. Richard Blechyndur, an Englishman who worked for the Far East Tea House, sat in his booth on a hot summer day trying to sell steaming cups of tea. No one was buying. He needed to do something, so he poured the tea over ice and served iced tea to thirsty customers.

Here's What You Need

SERVINGS: 4
Recipe requires adult help.

Ingredients
- [ ] 4 tea bags*
- [ ] 4½ cups (1 liter) water
- [ ] lemon
- [ ] milk
- [ ] sugar
- [ ] cookies
- [ ] tea sandwiches (see "Tasty Tidbits")

* Choose an English tea like Earl Grey or English breakfast. If you want to avoid caffeine, use a decaffeinated English tea or an herbal tea.

Equipment
- [ ] teapot
- [ ] measuring cup
- [ ] teakettle or medium-sized pot
- [ ] spoon
- [ ] 2 small plates
- [ ] cutting board
- [ ] knife
- [ ] small pitcher
- [ ] sugar bowl
- [ ] serving plate
- [ ] tablecloth
- [ ] 4 cups and saucers or mugs
- [ ] 4 spoons
- [ ] 4 plates
- [ ] napkins

tasty tidbits

Tea sandwiches are sandwiches with crusts removed that are cut into fourths and usually eaten at afternoon tea. Some traditional fillings are sliced cucumbers, cheese, egg salad, and cream cheese and jelly.

Here's What You Do

NOTE: *If you want to go with tradition, have your afternoon tea between 4:00 and 6:00 P.M.*

1 Place the tea bags in the teapot so that the paper tags (if any) are hanging out of the teapot's opening. Place the teapot in the sink.

2 Pour the water into the teakettle or pot, place it on the stove, and heat on high until the water boils. Then turn off the heat.

3 *Ask an adult* to pour the water into the teapot. Place the lid on the teapot.

4 Let the tea **steep** (soak in liquid) for about 5 minutes. Then remove the tea bags either by their tags or with a spoon and place them on one of the small plates. You can use them again for a second pot of tea.

5 Place the lemon on the cutting board and slice it in half and then in half again to make four wedges. Place these on the other small plate. Pour milk into the pitcher and sugar into the sugar bowl.

6 Arrange the cookies and tea sandwiches on the serving plate.

7 Now set the table. Some people around the world use very specific kinds of tablecloths when serving tea. The British use lace or a nicely ironed white tablecloth. The Gypsies use a paisley-print cloth. The Scottish use a plaid cloth, and the Irish use a linen cloth.

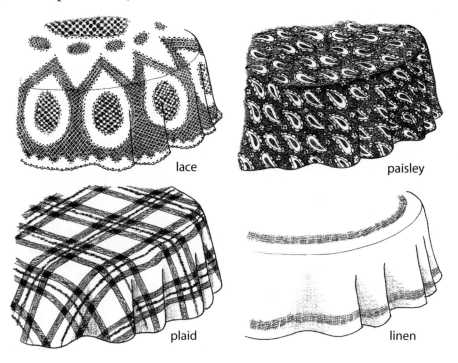

lace

paisley

plaid

linen

After laying out the tablecloth, place the cups, saucers, spoons, plates, napkins, sugar, milk, lemon wedges, and cookies and tea sandwiches on the table.

8 After everyone is seated, have your guests pass their cups to you. Ask your guests if they would like lemon or milk with their tea, since the two are never mixed. If they prefer milk, they can pour the milk in the cup before you pour the tea. Many people think it makes the tea taste better. Pour the tea into the cups and pass them back to your guests.

9 Offer your guests sugar.

10 Pass around the plate of cookies and tea sandwiches.

Culture Link

© 1995 Michael Hintlian

Russian Tea Ceremony

For more than 200 years, Russians have been enjoying their tea-drinking ritual. A necessary part of this ritual is the **samovar** (a metal container with a spigot used to boil water for tea). The samovar is the symbol of Russian hospitality. Many Russian families have two samovars, one for everyday use and a fancy samovar for special occasions. The village man pictured here is getting his samovar ready for his afternoon tea break.

Sweet Lassi

-INDIA-

People have been eating yogurt for more than 4,000 years! Yogurt is made from the milk of cows, sheep, or goats. The milk is mixed with a special kind of bacteria that change the milk into yogurt. We often mix yogurt with fruit to give it a sweet taste.

Cultures all over the world eat, drink, and cook with yogurt. In Greece, you might enjoy dipping sliced figs into yogurt that has been mixed with honey and then sprinkling the figs with nuts. In Afghanistan, you would spread a yogurt sauce mixed with mint and garlic on your grilled meat.

Not everyone calls yogurt by that name. The Armenian word for yogurt is *madzoon* (pronounced MAHD-zoon), the Egyptians call it *zabady* (pronounced zeh-BED-ee), and if you come from Turkey, you would call it *yoġurt* (pronounced YOH-vert).

Many people in India cook with yogurt almost every day. They make delicious curry sauces by mixing yogurt and spices. Another favorite in India is a delicious yogurt drink called sweet *lassi* (pronounced LAH-see). Many kids particularly enjoy drinking *lassi* on a hot summer day, but you may want to have this yummy yogurt drink at any time of the year.

COOKING UP SOME HISTORY

According to legend, King François I, who ruled France from 1515 to 1545, had bad intestinal problems in the early 1500s. No matter what the court physician tried, nothing seemed to work. So the king asked a friend for help. The friend sent one of his best servants, some sheep, and a secret recipe. The servant made up a batch of yogurt and gave it to the king, who ate the new concoction. Almost immediately, his intestinal problems went away.

Here's What You Need

SERVINGS: 2

Ingredients
- ☐ 1 cup (240 ml) plain yogurt
- ☐ 1 cup (240 ml) cold water
- ☐ 3 ice cubes
- ☐ 4 tablespoons (60 ml) sugar
- ☐ ¼ teaspoon (1 ml) rose water*
- ☐ ½ cup (120 ml) fresh fruit (optional)

Equipment
- ☐ blender
- ☐ measuring cup
- ☐ measuring spoons
- ☐ 2 drinking glasses

*You can buy rose water at an Indian or Middle Eastern food store. You can also find it in health food stores. Just make sure the rose water is food grade.

Here's What You Do

1 Pour the yogurt and the water into the blender.

2 Add the ice cubes, sugar, and rose water to the blender.

3 If you want to add fresh fruit, such as a mango, strawberries, or a banana, add it now. Cover the blender and blend for about 30 to 45 seconds. Then turn off the blender and pour the sweet *lassi* into the glasses.

Culture Link
Haitian Mango Smoothie

A smoothie is a refreshing drink made with yogurt or ice cream, fruit, juice, ice cubes, and sometimes honey. No one knows exactly where smoothies came from, but people in South America and on tropical islands have been enjoying these drinks for a long time. Kids from Haiti enjoy making smoothies from tropical fruits, such as mangoes, that grow on that island.

© 1999 Gary Braman

Hot Chocolate

-MEXICO-

Most people love chocolate. Some ancient Mexican civilizations even believed chocolate was a gift from the gods. Many historians now believe that the **Olmecs** (an ancient Central American civilization) may have been the first to make a chocolate beverage. The Olmecs lived in areas where **cacao** (tropical trees that produce a seed used to make chocolate, cocoa, and cocoa butter) grew, and the words *cacao* and *chocolate* may be traced to Olmec languages. Later, other ancient civilizations such as the Toltecs, Maya, and Aztecs, which lived in different parts of Mexico, also enjoyed drinking chocolate. Hernando Cortés, a Spanish explorer, first tasted chocolate when he conquered parts of what is now Mexico in 1519. He thought the drink tasted bitter, so when he brought some cocoa beans back to Spain in 1528, he made a new drink, adding vanilla and sugar and leaving out the chili peppers that were used in Mexican chocolate drinks. Cortés's hot chocolate started a rage that eventually spread throughout Europe and the rest of the world.

People in Italy make a chocolate bread using cocoa powder and chocolate chips. In Hungary, people pour warm chocolate syrup over pancakes, then sprinkle the pancakes with powdered sugar. In Sweden, a delicious chocolate sauce is spooned over small mounds of hard meringue (pronounced muh-RANG), which is a mixture of stiffly beaten egg whites and granulated sugar baked at a very low temperature until dry.

The ancient Maya and Aztecs used spices, chili peppers, and cornmeal to spice up their chocolate drink. Our rich version uses semisweet and milk chocolate and a little cinnamon.

COOKING UP SOME HISTORY

In 1828, a Dutch chemist and chocolate manufacturer named Coenraad Van Houten invented a way of making chocolate into powder. He reduced the fat from chocolate liqueur and made what was left into a hard cake. The cake could be crushed into a powder, which would dissolve easily in liquid. This started a whole new way to make hot chocolate.

Here's What You Need

SERVINGS: 2
Recipe requires adult help.

Ingredients

- ☐ 2 cups (480 ml) milk
- ☐ 2 ounces (56 g) semisweet baking chocolate squares
- ☐ 2 ounces (56 g) milk chocolate squares or morsels
- ☐ ground cinnamon *or* 2 cinnamon sticks
- ☐ additional milk (optional)

Equipment

- ☐ measuring cup
- ☐ medium-sized pot
- ☐ mixing spoon
- ☐ wire whisk
- ☐ mugs

 **tasty tidbits**

In Australia, kids drink *milo,* a chocolate-like drink made from a grain, sometimes adding a scoop of ice cream.

The Irish favor powdered hot chocolate mixes that are flavored with mint or orange.

In Canada, hot chocolate is often served with whipped cream and chocolate sprinkles.

To make their hot chocolate thick, people who live in northern Spain add cornstarch.

Here's What You Do

1 Pour the milk into the pot. Turn the heat to medium-high.

2 Break the chocolate squares into pieces and place them in the pot.

3 Stir constantly with the spoon. As the chocolate starts to melt, turn the heat down to medium, and continue to stir until the chocolate is completely melted. Turn off the heat.

4 **Whisk** (stir using a fast, circular motion) the chocolate milk with the wire whisk for about 30 seconds to 1 minute until foamy.

5 *Ask an adult* to pour the hot chocolate into the mugs. Sprinkle a little ground cinnamon on top or place a cinnamon stick in each mug and leave it in as you drink. Take a sip (careful, it's hot) and enjoy. If the hot chocolate is too rich, you can add some milk.

Stir using a fast, circular motion to whisk.

Culture Link

Swiss Chocolate Fondue

Another way to enjoy "hot" chocolate is to make chocolate fondue (pronounced fahn-DOO). The word *fondue* is from the French word *fondre*, which means "to melt," but this classic dish is from Switzerland. The dish was created to help promote Swiss chocolate. To make chocolate fondue, unsweetened chocolate squares are melted in a fondue pot with sugar, light cream, and butter. Then chunks of fresh fruit, such as strawberries, bananas, grapes, cherries, and apples, and pieces of cake are put on skewers and dipped into the warm chocolate mixture. The fondue pot sits on a small stand above a flame to keep the chocolate warm and liquid.

© 1999 Gary Braman

Ice Cream Soda

-UNITED STATES-

In the fall of 1874, the people of Philadelphia celebrated the fiftieth birthday of the **Franklin Institute** (an organization named for Benjamin Franklin that fosters the development of science and technology). Robert M. Green stood at his booth selling to thirsty customers a drink he made by mixing together carbonated water, syrup, and sweet cream. No one knows for sure whether Green ran out of cream or it turned sour, but he had to do something quick. He bought some vanilla ice cream from another vendor and put scoops of ice cream in the drink. The ice cream soda was born and soon everyone wanted one.

Cooking Up Some History

Mineral water (water from underground springs that has minerals and bubbles from carbon dioxide) has satisfied thirsts in Europe since the **Middle Ages** (a period in history from about A.D. 500 to A.D. 1500). But it wasn't until 1838 in Philadelphia that Eugene Roussel, an immigrant from France, mixed flavored syrup made from lemon juice and sugar with carbonated water to make the first soda.

There are many interesting combinations of ice cream and soda from different parts of the world. American favorites include a root beer float made with vanilla ice cream and root beer soda, and a cola float made with cola and cherry ice cream. In New Zealand, kids mix vanilla ice cream with raspberry "fizzy." Canadians enjoy cherry pop with soft vanilla ice cream. In Australia, people call ice cream sodas "spiders" and make them with vanilla ice cream and lime or cream soft drink.

You can make your own old-fashioned ice cream soda with any ice cream flavor and soda.

Here's What You Need

SERVINGS: 1

Ingredients

- [ ] 12-ounce (360-ml) can or bottle of cold soda
- [ ] 2 scoops of ice cream, any flavor

Equipment

- [ ] large glass
- [ ] ice cream scoop
- [ ] spoon
- [ ] straw

Here's What You Do

1 Pour the soda into the glass.

2 Place the ice cream in the glass.

3 Stir gently with the spoon. Put in the straw and enjoy.

What's in a **NAME**?

Here are some of the different names used for carbonated drinks:

soda   In 1750, a French doctor named Gabriel Venel made the first man-made mineral water. Since one of the ingredients was bicarbonate of soda, the drink became known as soda water.

pop   When soda water was first put into bottles, some bottles would explode because of the pressure the carbon dioxide created inside the bottle. Manufacturers soon found ways to seal the bottles with wire and cork. When opened, the bottles made a popping sound, so some people called soda water "pop." If you live in the Southern or Midwestern part of the United States, you might call your carbonated water "pop." People who live along the East and West Coasts call it soda.

fizzwater   With the popularity of soda water, manufacturers in the mid-1800s made machines called soda fountains. Soda fountains served soda water with flavored syrups and were placed on counters in drugstores. The drugstore counter, where you could also order food and other drinks, became known as the soda fountain. In the early days of the soda fountain, waitresses would call a customer's order in to the cook by giving it an unusual name. A bucket of mud was a large scoop of chocolate ice cream. A carbonated drink was known as fizzwater.

© 1999 Gary Braman

New York Egg Cream

Around 1890, Louis Auster decided to make a new kind of soda. He created the egg cream, which he sold to customers in his Brooklyn, N.Y., candy shop. No one knows for sure what Auster put in the soda to create this new taste, but one story is that he made a chocolate syrup from chocolate, eggs, and cream, and added the syrup to the soda. People still drink egg creams today, but these sodas can be hard to find. Try the soda aisle of your local grocery store.

PART TWO

Great Grains

Who can resist the smell and taste of warm baked bread? People have been baking bread since prehistoric times. The earliest bread was simply ground grain mixed with water and baked on hot stones. The Egyptians were the first to discover that **yeast** (a one-celled fungus) made bread rise, giving it a softer texture inside. The Greeks and Romans made a variety of breads, but the Romans were the first to produce bread commercially. They set up mill bakeries in Pompeii, where many loaves were baked at a time.

Bread comes in all shapes, sizes, and textures and from all cultures. Types of bread include waffles from Belgium; bagels from New York City; blini (pronounced BLEE-nee), thin pancakes from Russia; Christmas bread, a rich yeast bread from Greece; and chapatis (pronounced chah-PAH-teez) and nan (pronounced nahn), flat breads from India. All of these breads are delicious, no matter how you slice them.

Challah

Thick crusty loaves of bread taste great when you eat them warm right from the oven. When yeast is added to the dough, it makes the dough rise, or get bigger, and gives the bread a light, chewy texture.

25

COOKING UP SOME HISTORY

When early man discovered that the seeds of wheatgrass could be eaten, it wasn't long before he learned to mix the ground seeds with water to make an early form of bread. Early breads have been found in excavated Stone Age villages in Switzerland. But the ancient Egyptians were the first to discover—by accident—the secret of what makes bread rise. It may have happened like this: A baker had made up a batch of bread dough, but did not bake it right away. What he discovered when he went back to bake the bread was that the dough had risen while he was away. Yeast cells from the air had gotten into the dough, making it rise. This baked bread tasted much better than the usual flat breads. Today you can speed up the rising process by adding packets of dry yeast to bread dough.

Russian black bread gets its name from its ingredients, like molasses and coffee, which make the bread turn almost black when baked. Classic French bread is famous for its crispy crust. To get just the right crispness, bakers first bake the loaves in a moist oven, then finish baking in a dry oven.

On the Jewish Sabbath (pronounced SAH-bath), a holy day of rest lasting from sundown on Friday to sundown on Saturday, many people eat challah (pronounced HA-lah), a delicious sweet yeast bread made with or without raisins. The challah dough is formed into a braided loaf. During Rosh Hashanah (pronounced rush hah-SHAH-nah), or Jewish New Year, the bread has a round shape to symbolize the new year and a beginning and an end.

Here's What You Need

SERVINGS: 2 LOAVES

Ingredients

- [ ] 1 package active dry yeast
- [ ] 1/4 teaspoon (1 ml) sugar
- [ ] 1/4 cup (60 ml) warm water
- [ ] 4–5 cups (1–1.5 liters) flour
- [ ] 3/4 cup (180 ml) water
- [ ] 3/8 cup (90 ml) oil
- [ ] 1/2 cup (120 ml) sugar
- [ ] 1/2 tablespoon (7.5 ml) salt
- [ ] 3 eggs
- [ ] nonstick cooking spray
- [ ] poppy or sesame seeds (optional)

Equipment

- [ ] 2 small bowls
- [ ] measuring spoons
- [ ] measuring cup
- [ ] 2 large bowls
- [ ] fork
- [ ] electric mixer
- [ ] plastic wrap
- [ ] 2 clean dish towels
- [ ] baking sheet
- [ ] pastry brush
- [ ] wire rack

Here's What You Do

1 Place the yeast in one of the small bowls with the smaller amount of sugar and the warm water. *Make sure the water is not hot,* or it will kill the yeast. Let this mixture sit for about 15 minutes. It should start to foam and bubble.

2 In one of the large bowls, combine 2 cups (480 ml) of the flour, the water, the oil, the rest of the sugar, the salt, and two of the eggs. Crack the last egg into the other small bowl and beat lightly with the fork. Pour about half of this egg into the large bowl with the other ingredients. Save the other half of the egg for later. Keep it in the refrigerator until needed. Use the electric mixer to mix the ingredients in the large bowl well.

3 Add the yeast mixture to the batter and mix on low speed for a minute or so. Gradually add 2¼ more cups (540 ml) of flour, mixing well after each addition.

4 Place the dough on a clean, flat surface and **knead** (squeeze, press, or roll with the hands) the dough for about 10 to 15 minutes until it is smooth and elastic. As you knead the dough, if it still feels sticky add small amounts of the last ¾ cup (180 ml) of flour, adding only what you need for the dough to feel smooth and elastic. Do not add the entire last ¾ cup (180 ml) of flour.

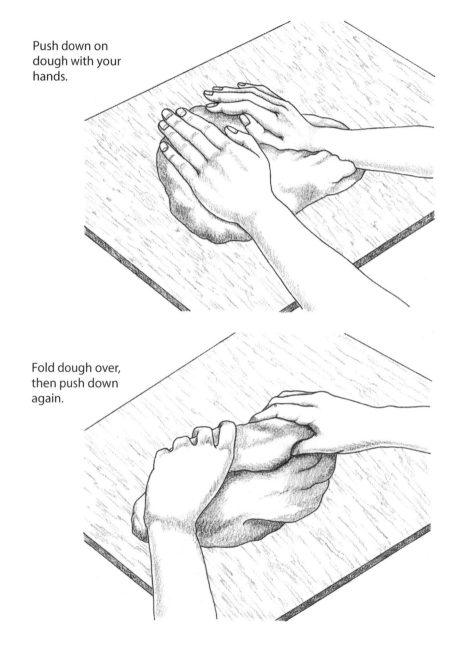

Push down on dough with your hands.

Fold dough over, then push down again.

5 Lightly spray the inside of the other large bowl with nonstick cooking spray. Place the dough in the bowl, then turn the dough over so the entire surface of the dough is coated with cooking spray.

6 Lightly cover the bowl with a piece of plastic wrap, then cover the plastic wrap with one of the clean dish towels. Let the dough rise for about 1½ hours, or until it has doubled in size.

7 Spray the baking sheet with nonstick cooking spray and set aside. When the dough is ready, punch the dough down in the center, then place it on the clean surface and knead it for a few minutes.

8 Divide the dough in half to make a round loaf and a braided loaf of challah. For the round loaf, place half the dough on one side of the baking sheet and form the dough into a round shape.

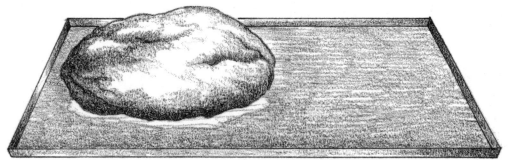

9 For the braided loaf, divide the last half of the dough into three equal pieces. Braided Jewish challah actually is braided using four strands of dough. But you will make an easier braid using three strands. Roll each piece into the shape of a long strand about 12 inches (30.5 cm) long, then braid the three strands together on the other side of the baking sheet following these steps:

a. Lay the three strands side by side on the baking sheet, but not touching. Pinch the tops of the strands together at one end.

b. Bring the left strand over the middle strand.

c. Bring the right strand over the middle strand (which was the left strand). Continue by bringing the left strand over the middle strand, then the right strand over the middle strand, until you reach the bottom of the strands.

d. Pinch the ends of the three strands together.

Lightly cover both loaves with the plastic wrap that has been sprayed with nonstick cooking spray, then the two dish towels, and let rise until doubled in size, about 1½ hours.

10 Preheat the oven to 325°F (165°C). When the dough has doubled in size, slowly remove the plastic wrap and the towels. Gently brush each loaf with the remaining beaten egg. Sprinkle some poppy seeds or sesame seeds on each loaf, if you'd like. Place the bread in the oven and bake about 40 minutes, or until done.

11 When it is finished, remove the bread from the oven and place the loaves on the wire rack to cool.

Pueblo Oven Bread

Pueblo oven bread is a Southwestern Native American classic and is still baked as it was long ago—in an outdoor **adobe** (sun-dried brick made of clay and straw) oven, called a *horno*. This dome-shaped oven bakes the bread perfectly without any electricity. Women make a hot fire in the oven, then let it burn out. This makes the inside of the oven very hot. The ashes are shoveled out so the bread can be placed inside and baked.

© 1999
Gary Braman

Injera

Have you ever eaten flat bread? You probably have if you've eaten tacos, pita bread, or crêpes. They come from different cultures, but they are all thin, pancake-like breads. Most, but not all, flat breads are made without yeast, which is why they stay flat. Flat breads are most often used as wrappers for holding meat and/or vegetables.

Middle Eastern pita bread can be wrapped around your favorite foods or cut in half and the food stuffed in the pita's pocket. If the pita has a pocket, it usually means the bread was made with yeast. In Mexico and Central America, soft tortillas (pronounced tohr-TEE-ahs) are usually filled with shredded meat, cheese, chicken, or beans.

In Ethiopia, a country in northern Africa, a thin, soft, spongy bread called *injera* (pronounced in-JEER-ah) is used as a utensil. A variety of dishes such as spicy meat curry, lentils, and chicken are brought to the table in a large, shallow bowl. Everyone tears off a piece of *injera* and uses it to scoop up the food. *Injera* is easy to make. You can use *injera* to pick up some food, wrap it around your favorite lunch food, or just eat it by itself.

Here's What You Need

SERVINGS: ABOUT 6 *INJERA*
Recipe requires adult help.

Ingredients

- 1¼ cups (300 ml) flour
- 1 teaspoon (5 ml) salt
- 1 teaspoon (5 ml) baking soda
- 2 cups (480 ml) warm water
- 1 tablespoon (15 ml) club soda
- nonstick cooking spray

Equipment

- measuring cup
- measuring spoons
- food blender
- medium-sized bowl
- rubber spatula
- paper towels
- plate
- griddle or frying pan
- soup ladle
- flat spatula
- wire rack

Here's What You Do

1 Put the flour, salt, and baking soda in the blender. Add the water and blend slowly at first, then use a higher speed until the mixture is well blended. Check to make sure the flour isn't getting stuck at the bottom of the blender.

2 Pour the mixture into the bowl. Use the rubber spatula to scrape all the mixture out of the blender.

3 Add the club soda to the mixture and stir, using the spatula.

4 Place a paper towel on the plate and set the plate aside.

5 Spray the **griddle** (a flat pan used for frying) with non-stick cooking spray. Heat the griddle on medium.

6 Wait a few minutes until the griddle is hot, then scoop up some batter with the ladle and pour it onto the griddle. *Have an adult* immediately swirl the griddle so the batter covers the surface evenly. Don't make the *injera* too thick.

Swirl griddle so batter coats entire surface.

10 Have yourself an Ethiopian feast with dishes such as *doro watt* (pronounced DOOR-oh waht), chicken stewed in red pepper sauce; *yebeg kaey watt* (pronounced YEH-beg k'EYE waht), a lamb stew; *kitfo* (pronounced KIHT-foh), minced beef seasoned with chili powder; and shrimp sautéed with onions. Or just eat the *injera* with any of your favorite foods.

7 Cook until the top of the batter looks dry and the edges start to curl.

8 Use the flat spatula to lift the *injera* off the griddle. Place the *injera* on the wire rack to cool. Start cooking the next *injera*. While it is cooking, move the *injera* that is on the rack to the plate with the paper towel.

9 Continue cooking until all the batter is used up, placing each cooked *injera* first on the wire rack to cool, then on the plate. Stack the *injera* one on top of the other.

Armenian *Lavash*

In Armenia, in the southern Caucasus of Eastern Europe, people eat *lavash* (pronounced lah-vahsh), a thin bread with a somewhat tough texture. *Lavash* is served at every meal. One way to eat *lavash* is to put a piece of the bread on a plate, then place kebab meats on the bread. The juices from the meat soak into the bread, making a delicious meal. Another way to eat *lavash* is to place greens, such as dill, parsley, and basil, and some goat cheese on a strip of the bread, roll it up, and eat it with the main meal. The village woman shown here is baking *lavash* the old-fashioned way, by placing the dough over the outside of a hot barrel.

© 1995 Michael Hintlian

Coconut Bread

-JAMAICA-

Quick breads get their name from the ease with which they are made. They are simple to prepare and they don't need a lot time to rise the way yeast breads do. Just mix a few ingredients and bake. Instead of yeast, baking soda or baking powder is used to make quick breads rise in the oven. Quick breads can be made with many different ingredients, such as fruits, cheeses, nuts, herbs, oats, and vegetables. Banana bread, muffins, breadsticks, and biscuits are just a few of the many types of quick bread.

The Portuguese make a tasty, sweet quick bread called *pao doce* (pronounced PAY-oh DOH-chey) out of flour, sugar, lots of spices, and mashed potatoes. Irish soda bread is a favorite quick bread in Ireland. The buttermilk gives this bread an interesting taste, and the bread's name comes from the baking soda used in the recipe.

Kids who live in the Caribbean islands might start their day with gingerbread pancakes, sweet potato waffles, or banana-stuffed French toast. Jamaican kids love to munch on coconut bread in the morning and throughout the day.

COOKING UP SOME HISTORY

Have you ever heard the term "a baker's dozen"? It means that you get 13 of something instead of the usual 12 when you order a dozen. It got started in medieval England after 1266, when a law was decreed that stated how much a loaf of bread should weigh. Bakers could go to jail if they cheated the customer by selling an underweight order of bread. So when the customer ordered a dozen loaves, bakers tossed in an extra loaf just to be on the safe side. Some bakers still do this today, but mostly with small items, like cookies.

Here's What You Need

SERVINGS: 1 LOAF

Ingredients

- [ ] 2 cups (480 ml) flour
- [ ] 1½ teaspoons (7.5 ml) baking powder
- [ ] ½ teaspoon (2.5 ml) salt
- [ ] ⅓ cup (90 ml) softened butter or margarine
- [ ] ⅔ cup (180 ml) sugar
- [ ] 2 eggs
- [ ] ½ cup (120 ml) milk
- [ ] 1 cup (240 ml) sweetened, flaked coconut
- [ ] nonstick cooking spray

Equipment

- [ ] measuring cup
- [ ] measuring spoons
- [ ] medium bowl
- [ ] mixing spoon
- [ ] mixing bowl
- [ ] electric mixer
- [ ] rubber spatula
- [ ] loaf pan, 5 × 9 inches (13 × 23 cm)
- [ ] dull knife
- [ ] wire rack
- [ ] bread knife

Here's What You Do

1 Preheat the oven to 350°F (175°C).

2 Pour the flour, baking powder, and salt into the medium bowl. Mix well with the spoon and set aside.

3 Place the softened butter and the sugar in the mixing bowl and mix with the electric mixer on low to medium speed until well blended.

4 Add the eggs one at a time and mix well. Then add the milk and mix again. Use the spatula to scrape the sides of the bowl between mixings.

5 Add the flour mixture to the mixing bowl. Mix on low speed until blended, then mix on medium speed until well blended, about a minute or so.

6 Add the coconut and stir gently by hand with the spoon until the flakes are all mixed in.

7 Spray the loaf pan with nonstick cooking spray. Pour the batter into the pan, using the spatula to scrape the sides of the bowl.

8 Put the pan in the oven and bake for about 55 to 65 minutes. Check by inserting the blade of the dull knife into the center of the bread. If it comes out completely clean, the bread is done. If it is not completely clean, bake for about 5 to 10 minutes more, checking again after each 5 minutes of baking.

9 Cool the bread in the pan about 5 minutes. Then place the bread on the wire rack to cool.

10 Cut into slices and serve. This bread is sweet, so you won't need to spread anything on it.

Scottish Dropped Scones

In the United Kingdom (England, Northern Ireland, Scotland, and Wales), scones (pronounced skohns) are a traditional type of bread to eat with afternoon tea. In Scotland, they are called drop or dropped scones, because the batter is dropped on a griddle and cooked, or dropped on a pan and baked in the oven. Fruit, nuts, and grated coconut are often added to the batter before baking. Scones are best eaten warm and spread with jam.

© 1999 Gary Braman

PART THREE

Soups and Starters

Many people around the world begin a meal with a small serving of food, which we call the first course or appetizer. Any kind of food, like soup, salad, bread and cheese, dips or spreads, chicken wings, or egg rolls, can be eaten as appetizers, as long as the portions are small. Nobody knows exactly when people started eating appetizers, but we know that people in ancient civilizations such as China and Japan as far back as 3000 B.C. ate appetizers. By 350 B.C., the ancient Greeks were eating dolmas and the ancient Romans enjoyed *gustotio,* which were appetizers and relishes. Food historians believe that this custom of eating small portions of food before the main meal eventually made its way to Europe, where hosts served small portions of food before the main meal to guests who had traveled far.

People everywhere eat appetizers. Mexican kids enjoy avocado soup made with chicken broth, light cream, and avocado. All of the ingredients are **puréed** (blended to a thick consistency) and the resulting soup is eaten chilled. If you go to Venezuela, you might enjoy *tostones* (pronounced tohs-TOHN-ehs), slices of fried **plantains** (tropical fruit similar to bananas), before your meal. Descendants of German immigrants, who settled in southeastern Pennsylvania in the early 1700s, make baked lima beans using yellow limas, catsup, and brown sugar. In Japan, **miso** (soybean paste) soup is eaten with a spoon or sipped right from the bowl.

The recipes in this section will give you some great starters for any meal.

Strawberry Soup

-POLAND-

What do you think of when you hear the word *soup?* Most people think of a steaming bowl of broth and vegetables or meat. But hot soups are not the only kind of soups people eat. Chilled soups made with vegetables, fruits, yogurt, cream, herbs, and even nuts are also enjoyed all around the world. Especially on hot summer days, chilled soups taste great.

During Shavuoth (pronounced shih-VOOTH *or* shi-VOO-iss), about seven weeks after Passover, some Jews eat a cold cherry soup made with tart cherries, sugar, and spices such as cinnamon, allspice, and cloves. In the Andalusia (pronounced on-dah-loo-THEE-ah) province of Spain, everyone loves a chilled soup called gazpacho (pronounced gahz-SPOTCH-oh). This yummy soup, made with vegetables and moist bread, is puréed and chilled for at least 12 hours before eating.

COOKING UP SOME HISTORY

In the early 1900s, a chef named Louis Diat worked at the Ritz-Carlton Hotel in New York City. He had made *potage parmentier* (pronounced poh-tahj pahr-mohn-chee-ay), a famous French leek and potato soup, many times. But one day, he added cream and chilled the soup. The patrons at the restaurant loved it and vichyssoise (pronounced vee-she-swahz) was born.

Polish children love eating bowls of cold soup made from vegetables or fruits. *Barszcz* (pronounced BOORSHt), a cold beet soup, is tasty, but most kids love strawberry soup because it is sweet. Some kids actually drink it out of a glass.

Here's What You Need

SERVINGS: 4

Ingredients
- [ ] 1 pound (454 g) fresh strawberries
- [ ] 1³/₄ cups (420 ml) water
- [ ] 3 tablespoons (45 ml) sugar
- [ ] 1 tablespoon (15 ml) lemon juice
- [ ] 1 cup (240 ml) light cream

Equipment
- [ ] knife
- [ ] cutting board
- [ ] medium-sized pot
- [ ] measuring cup
- [ ] wooden spoon
- [ ] blender
- [ ] measuring spoons

Here's What You Do

1 Wash the strawberries, cut off the green tops, then slice the strawberries and place them in the pot with the water.

2 Bring the strawberries to a boil on high heat, then simmer on medium heat for about 30 minutes. Stir occasionally.

3 Let the mixture cool, then pour it into the blender and purée the mixture.

4 Pour the purée back into the pot. Add the sugar, lemon juice, and light cream and stir. Simmer on medium heat for a few minutes.

5 Let cool completely, then chill the soup in the refrigerator for a few hours before serving.

What do people eat with their chilled soups?

In Denmark, oat cakes are served with *kaernemaelkskolkskaal* (pronounced KEHR-neh-MELK-skolk-skol), a cold buttermilk soup.

In Poland, some people pour strawberry soup over cooked egg noodles.

In the United States, chopped chives are sprinkled on vichyssoise.

In Israel, *marak peirot* (pronounced mah-RAHK pay-ROTE), a chilled fruit soup, is topped with sour cream.

In Turkey, kids eat pita bread with *cacik* (pronounced jah-JEWK), a cold cucumber soup.

Culture Link

Madzoon Ahboorh

On hot summer days in Yerevan, Armenia, when the temperature soars past 100ºF (40ºC), people enjoy eating refreshing bowls of cold *madzoon ahboorh* (pronounced MAHD-zoon ahh-boo-rrrh), a chilled soup made with yogurt, water, lots of garlic, and dill.

© 1999
Gary Braman

Black Bean Soup

-CUBA-

Bean soups have a long history. As far back as 600 B.C., people in ancient Greece ate bean soups and even bought warm bowls of this delicious soup from street vendors.

Cooking Up Some History

Apicius, a Roman who lived during the first century, wrote the earliest cookbook that still exists today. He loved using expensive, rare foods, such as cranes and tongues of songbirds, in his creations, and made thick barley and bean soups and a puréed soup of lettuce leaves and onions.

In modern cultures, bean soups are still very popular. The Lebanese eat a delicious puréed soup called *shourbet fassoolia byda* (pronounced SHOWER-bah fah-soh-LEE-ah BY-dah) made with white beans and onions. In Italy, people enjoy a tasty soup called minestrone (pronounced mee-neh-STROH-nay) that is made with pasta, mushrooms, onions, bacon, and *cannellini,* which are white beans.

Cuba, an island in the Caribbean Sea, is famous for its black bean soup, or *frijoles negros* (pronounced free-HOE-lehs NEH-grows). Beans are a **staple** (main food source) in the Cuban diet and are eaten almost every day. Black bean soup usually starts the main meal, which is eaten around 2:00 P.M. If you use dry beans, this luscious soup has to be made over two days because the beans have to soak. But you can use canned beans for this recipe.

Here's What You Need

SERVINGS: 6

Ingredients

- [ ] two 19-ounce (538-g) cans black beans
- [ ] 1 medium yellow onion
- [ ] 2 cloves of garlic
- [ ] 1 green pepper
- [ ] 2 tablespoons (30 ml) olive oil
- [ ] 1 teaspoon (10 ml) salt
- [ ] 1/2 teaspoon (2.5 ml) ground pepper
- [ ] 1/4 teaspoon (1 ml) oregano
- [ ] 1 tablespoon (15 ml) sugar
- [ ] 1/2–1 cup (120–240 ml) water (optional)
- [ ] 1–2 tablespoons (15–30 ml) olive oil

Equipment

- [ ] large pot with lid
- [ ] wooden spoon
- [ ] cutting board
- [ ] sharp knife
- [ ] measuring spoons
- [ ] large frying pan
- [ ] small plate
- [ ] fork
- [ ] measuring cup

Here's What You Do

1 Pour the beans, along with the liquid in the cans, into the large pot. Stir with the wooden spoon, then heat on low. Stir occasionally while you prepare the vegetables.

2 Use the cutting board when preparing all vegetables. Peel the onion and chop into small pieces. Peel the garlic and **mince** (cut into very small pieces). Rinse the green pepper, cut off the stem, cut the green pepper in half, and remove the seeds. Chop the green pepper into small pieces. Set the vegetables aside.

3 Add the 2 tablespoons (30 ml) of olive oil to the frying pan and heat the oil on medium for a few minutes. Add the onions, garlic, and green pepper to the pan and **sauté** (fry lightly in fat), moving them around the pan with the wooden spoon until the onions are tender, about a few minutes. Turn off the heat.

Move food around in pan with spoon to sauté.

4 With the wooden spoon, scoop out a few spoonfuls of the black beans and place them on the small plate. Mash these with the fork. Then add the mashed beans to the sautéed vegetables. Stir to mix together.

5 Place this mixture into the pot with the beans, then add the salt, ground pepper, oregano, and sugar and stir. Add the water only if the soup is too thick. Cover the pot and cook the soup on medium-low to medium heat for about 30 to 45 minutes. The soup should just simmer, so adjust the heat as needed. Check and stir the soup occasionally.

6 When the soup is ready, stir in the remaining olive oil, and taste a little of the soup. Adjust the seasonings if needed.

Beans come in lots of sizes, shapes, and colors and are enjoyed all over the world. Some cultural favorites include pinto beans in Mexico and South America, kidney beans in the Southwestern and Southern United States, cranberry beans in Italy, and black beans in the Caribbean and South America.

Culture Link

Chili con Carne

Long before Spanish explorers arrived in Mexico, the Aztecs ate *aji* (pronounced AH-hee), a very hot chili made with a variety of hot chili peppers, vegetables, and meat, such as deer. The Spanish called this dish chili con carne, which means "chili with meat." When the Spanish brought cattle to the New World, people used beef in their chili. Kids in the American Southwest also love chili. Texans call this dish a "bowl of red" and never put beans in it, but chili in most other parts of the country does include beans.

© 1999 Gary Braman

Baba Ghanouj and Hummus

—LEBANON AND GREECE—

Appetizers are sometimes called "finger foods" because many may be eaten without utensils. But an appetizer really can be almost anything! The most important ingredient for any appetizer menu is variety.

What's in a NAME?

The word *appetizer* was used for the first course because the small amounts of food are meant to stimulate the appetite. Other countries have other names for the first course of a meal.

In France, the hors d'oeuvres (pronounced or dervs) include escargot (pronounced ehs-kahr-goh), or snails, and *Brie en croûte* (pronounced bree ahn kroot), which is a soft, creamy cheese wrapped in pastry and baked.

In Italy, the antipasti (pronounced ahn-tee-PAHS-tee) are often split into selections of hot or cold preparations of vegetables, cheeses, and meats.

In Hawaii, the pupu (pronounced POO-poo) include macadamia nuts and barbecued meats.

In Poland, the *zakaski* (pronounced zah-KAH-skee) include pickled mushrooms and marinated herring.

In Spain, the tapas (pronounced TAH-pahs) include spiced pork, snails in hot sauce with garlic, and potato omelette.

cream cheese, lemon juice, and spices, is spread on French bread or crackers and eaten before the main meal.

In Lebanon it is traditional to have an appetizer course, called *mezza* (pronounced MEH-zuh), that can last for hours. People talk, dance, and nibble on foods such as feta cheese, meat pies, homemade cream cheese called *lebnah* (pronounced LEHB-nuh), squash with garlic, and a salad of parsley, ground wheat, tomatoes, and mint called tabouli (pronounced tah-BOO-lee). Pita bread is always served and is torn into small pieces and used to scoop up many of the *mezza* dishes. A similar tradition is enjoyed in Greece. People eat *mesedakia* (pronounced meh-zeh-DAH-kee-yah), such as pickled squid and stuffed grape leaves, before their main meal. You can have your own *mezza* when you make these two delicious foods, Lebanese baba ghanouj (pronounced bah-bah huh-NEWSH) and Greek hummus (pronounced HOOM-uhs).

Teahouses throughout China serve people tasty appetizers such as steamed or fried crab meat, **dim sum** (a variety of dishes including steamed or fried dumplings, shrimp balls, steamed buns, and Chinese pastries), and chili spare ribs. In Quebec, a province of eastern Canada, smoked mackerel pâté (pronounced pah-tay), a mixture of mackerel,

COOKING UP SOME HISTORY

The **Vikings** (Norwegian explorers who lived from A.D. 700 to A.D. 1000) may have started the smorgasbord (pronounced SMOHR-guhs-bohrd), which we also refer to as a buffet—a variety of hot and cold foods placed on a table where guests serve themselves. When the Vikings returned from their long sea voyages, they brought back many different foods from the lands they visited. But they never had enough of any one food to feed everyone an entire meal. They served the food buffet style so that everyone got a small taste of each food.

Lebanese Baba Ghanouj

Here's What You Need

SERVINGS: 6

Ingredients
- 1 large eggplant
- 2 cloves of garlic
- salt to taste
- 3 tablespoons (45 ml) tahini*
- 1 tablespoon (15 ml) lemon juice
- paprika
- 1 tablespoon (15 ml) olive oil
- pita bread

Equipment
- cutting board
- knife
- fork
- baking sheet
- spoon
- blender
- garlic press
- measuring spoons
- bowl

*Tahini is a thick paste made from ground sesame seeds. It can be found in Middle Eastern markets, health food stores, and some supermarkets.

Here's What You Do

1 Preheat the oven to 350°F (175°C).

2 Place the eggplant on the cutting board and cut off the stem. Poke holes in the eggplant with the fork and place the eggplant on the baking sheet.

3 Bake for about 45 minutes. Remove the eggplant from the oven and let it cool completely.

4 Cut the eggplant in half lengthwise and use the spoon to scoop out the insides. Place the insides in the blender.

5 Peel the garlic and crush it using the garlic press. Put it in the blender and sprinkle in some salt.

6 Add the tahini and lemon juice to the blender.

7 Put the cover on the blender and blend in quick short spurts until the mixture is blended. You don't want to overblend the mixture or it will be too smooth. Taste the mixture and add some salt if needed.

8 Place the mixture in the bowl, sprinkle on some paprika, and drizzle the olive oil over the top.

9 Tear the pita bread into pieces to scoop up the baba ghanouj.

Greek Hummus

Here's What You Need

SERVINGS: 6

Ingredients

- [ ] 19-ounce (538-g) can chickpeas
- [ ] 3 cloves of garlic
- [ ] juice of ½ lemon
- [ ] ¼ teaspoon (1 ml) pepper
- [ ] ⅓ cup (90 ml) canola or olive oil
- [ ] pinch of cumin (optional)
- [ ] 2 tablespoons (30 ml) water
- [ ] pita bread

Equipment

- [ ] colander
- [ ] blender
- [ ] knife
- [ ] garlic press
- [ ] measuring spoons
- [ ] measuring cup
- [ ] rubber spatula
- [ ] serving bowl

Here's What You Do

1 Drain the chickpeas using the colander and place them in the blender.

2 Peel the garlic and crush it using the garlic press, then place the garlic and the rest of the ingredients except the pita bread in the blender. Blend together until smooth.

3 Use the spatula to scoop out the hummus into the serving bowl.

4 Tear the pita bread into pieces to scoop up the hummus.

tasty tidbits At your *mezza* you can also serve black and green olives, cheese, and cut-up raw vegetables, such as carrots, broccoli, cucumber, and celery. You can use the vegetables, as well as the pita bread, to scoop up the baba ghanouj and hummus.

Mediterranean Aioli

The people in Italy, Spain, France, and other countries along the shores of the Mediterranean Sea make a delicious food called aioli (pronounced ay-OH-lee). In Provence, a region of southern France, people dip vegetables, and in parts of Spain they dip fried potatoes, in this tasty garlic mayonnaise.

© 1999 Gary Braman

PART FOUR

The Main Event

A main dish often includes some type of meat, chicken, or fish, but it can also be vegetarian, containing only vegetables with rice or beans. Many people in the United States eat their main dish at dinner, or supper, usually in the evening at around 6 o'clock. But in many European countries, such as Spain, the main dish is eaten at noon.

The **Berbers** (aboriginal peoples of North Africa who make up a large part of the populations of Libya, Algeria, and Morocco, most of whom make a living as farmers, though some are nomadic) make a delicious dish called *khalota* (pronounced ha-LOH-tah), with potatoes, green beans, eggplant, fava beans, and spices. People in Norway eat a dish called *ovnstekt torsk* (pronounced UH-vehn-shtehkt torshk), which is cod baked in milk and butter. Inuit kids from Canada love reindeer stew made with reindeer meat and vegetables.

The recipes in this section will give you a taste of the many main dishes from other cultures.

Saffron Meatballs and Rice

-SPAIN-

People all around the world prepare their foods in various interesting shapes and sizes. One of the most popular shapes is a ball. Meatballs can be made from beef, pork, lamb, turkey, chicken, or other meats that have been ground or chopped and mixed with spices and bread crumbs. Meatballs also can be vegetarian, containing a mixture of vegetables, rice, and/or beans.

Italian and American kids love to eat spaghetti and meatballs smothered with tomato sauce and Parmesan cheese. Kids in Korea eat meatballs, too, but not with spaghetti. They eat their meatballs steamed in an egg **custard** (a pudding-like food made with milk and eggs). This dish, called *al jjim* (pronounced ahl jim), is served with white rice. Cooks in Sweden use ground beef and pork to make a dish called Swedish meatballs, which is served with gravy and mashed potatoes. Moroccan meatballs are made with meat, rice, and spices, such as cinnamon and saffron, and served with green vegetables and salad.

tasty tidbits

Meat isn't the only food that is shaped into balls.

In Hungary, people eat potato dumplings with their main meal.

In England, during high tea, people eat fish cakes that are made in the shape of a ball.

In some Southern states in the United States, hush puppies are balls made with corn-meal and deep-fried. They supposedly got their name because cooks would toss scraps of this food to barking dogs and say, "Hush, puppy!"

A favorite main dish in the La Mancha region of central Spain is **saffron** (a yellow spice used to flavor and color food) meatballs. Made with ground pork or veal or a combination of the two, these meatballs are eaten with saffron gravy and served over rice.

COOKING UP SOME HISTORY

Ground beef also can be made into flat, round patties. You know this food—hamburgers. The Hamburg "steak," which originated in Germany, was a cooked patty of chopped beef. Americans first served a hamburger between two slices of bread at the 1904 World's Fair in St. Louis.

Here's What You Need

SERVINGS: 4
Recipe requires adult help.

Ingredients
- ¼ cup (60 ml) flour
- 1 pound (454 g) lean ground beef
- 1 egg
- 1 teaspoon (5 ml) salt
- ½ teaspoon (2.5 ml) pepper
- ½ teaspoon (2.5 ml) garlic powder
- ¾ cup (180 ml) plain bread crumbs
- ½ cup (120 ml) vegetable oil
- 3–4 cups (720–960 ml) water
- ¼ teaspoon (1 ml) saffron threads, crushed
- salt, pepper, and garlic powder to taste
- rice

Equipment
- 2 plates
- measuring cup
- measuring spoons
- large bowl
- wooden spoon
- ruler
- large frying pan
- spoon with holes
- large saucepan
- wire whisk

Here's What You Do

1 Place the flour on one of the plates and set aside.

2 Put the meat, egg, salt, pepper, garlic powder, and bread crumbs in the bowl and mix using the wooden spoon until well blended.

3 First shape the mixture into balls about 1 inch (2.5 cm) in diameter. Then roll each meatball in the flour and place it on the other plate. Don't throw the remaining flour away. You will use it later.

4 Pour the oil into the frying pan and heat on medium for a few minutes until the oil is hot. *Ask an adult* to put the meatballs in the frying pan and help you cook the meatballs. Let the meatballs brown on one side for a few minutes, then turn them over using the spoon with holes so the entire surface gets browned. The meatballs do not have to be completely cooked. Use the spoon with holes to remove the browned meatballs and place them in the saucepan.

5 Add the remaining flour to the frying pan. Whisk until blended, and cook for a minute or so until lightly browned, continuing to whisk.

6 *Ask an adult* to slowly add 3½ cups (840 ml) water to the frying pan. This will create steam, so keep your face away from the frying pan. Whisk until blended. Add the crushed saffron, and more salt, pepper, and garlic powder to taste. Turn the burner up to high until the mixture comes to a boil, stirring constantly. Lower the heat to medium and simmer for about 5 minutes.

Roll each meatball in flour.

Place meatballs on plate.

7 *Ask an adult* to pour the sauce into the saucepan with the meatballs. Bring the sauce to a boil on medium-high heat, then reduce the heat to medium-low and simmer for 20 minutes, stirring occasionally. The sauce will thicken a bit more as it cooks with the meatballs. If the sauce gets too thick, add the remaining water. The sauce should be at a constant simmer. Adjust the heat as needed.

8 While the meatballs are simmering, cook the rice, following the directions on the box.

9 Adjust the seasonings if you need to, then serve the saffron meatballs over the rice.

© 1999 Gary Braman

Culture Link

Falafel

Meals in Saudi Arabia include tasty dishes like bean salads, lentils and rice, and vegetables stuffed with ground lamb and beef. Falafel (pronounced feh-LAH-fehl) is another favorite. This ball-shaped food is made with chickpeas, fava beans, onions, garlic, sesame seeds, and lots of spices. Falafel can be eaten as part of the main meal, stuffed in pita bread, or eaten as a snack.

Kushiyaki

—JAPAN—

For thousands of years, people have been cooking pieces of meat and vegetables on sticks over open fires. Eventually, each culture developed traditional recipes for **marinades** (seasoned liquids in which foods like meat, fish, and vegetables are soaked to absorb the flavor of the liquid) and for dipping sauces. In Turkey, early **nomads** (wanderers with no permanent home) called the **skewers** (pointed sticks used for cooking) and the meat and vegetable dishes cooked on them "kebabs."

COOKING UP SOME HISTORY

To barbecue food means to grill food. When the Spanish arrived in Hispaniola, an island in the Caribbean, which is now half Haiti and half Dominican Republic, the Carib Indians were grilling food using a wood grid over a hot fire. The Spanish called this cooking method *barbacoa* (pronounced bahd-bah-COH-ah), and soon everyone wanted to barbecue, or grill, their food.

tasty tidbits

Here are some favorite cultural kebabs:

In India, *shammi* kebabs are made with lamb and spices such as ginger, cloves, and red chili powder.

In Vietnam, skewers of chicken, pork, pineapples, mushrooms, tomatoes, and peppers, called *kim tien ke* (pronounced keem tayen kay), are a favorite dish.

In Malaysia, thin slices of lamb are soaked overnight in a spicy marinade of chilis, ginger, garlic, and fish sauce, then grilled to make lamb satay.

Kids from Adana (pronounced ah-DOHN-ah), Turkey, eat chopped lamb and roasted pepper Adana kebabs, named after the city. In Japan, tuna is **marinated** (soaked) in soy sauce and scallion chunks before grilling on skewers. Take a trip to Java and you'll munch on tasty pork **satay** (small cubes of meat placed on skewers and grilled or broiled) dipped in a spicy peanut sauce.

Kids in Japan enjoy eating *kushiyaki* (pronounced koo-shee-YAH-kee), a food that is **broiled** (cooked directly above or below a heat source) on skewers. Cooks use only the freshest vegetables, fish, beef, and chicken when making *kushiyaki*. And rice is always served. Japanese kids create their *kushiyaki* by mixing cubes of beef, chicken, and shrimp and their favorite vegetables on skewers before broiling.

Here's What You Need

Servings: 2
Recipe requires adult help.

Ingredients

- [ ] 2 tablespoons (30 ml) soy sauce
- [ ] 1 tablespoon (15 ml) sugar
- [ ] $1/4$ teaspoon (1 ml) fresh ginger, grated
- [ ] $1/2$ tablespoon (7.5 ml) vegetable oil
- [ ] 4 large fresh shrimp
- [ ] $1/2$ boneless chicken breast, cut into 4 pieces
- [ ] beef cubes, about 4
- [ ] variety of vegetables, such as mushrooms, bell peppers, onions, zucchini, and cherry tomatoes
- [ ] rice

Equipment

- [ ] measuring spoons
- [ ] medium-sized bowl
- [ ] food grater
- [ ] wire whisk
- [ ] cutting board
- [ ] knife
- [ ] 4 metal or wooden skewers
- [ ] vegetable peeler (optional)
- [ ] broiling pan
- [ ] food brush
- [ ] outdoor grill (optional)
- [ ] 2 plates
- [ ] fork

Here's What You Do

1 Put the soy sauce and sugar into the bowl. Grate and measure the ginger and place it in the bowl, then add the oil. Whisk together until blended. This is your marinade.

2 Place the shrimp on the cutting board. Peel the shells off the shrimp. Using the knife, make a slit down the curved back part of the shrimp. Remove and discard the black vein.

3 Rinse the shrimp under cool water, shake off the excess water, then place them in the marinade along with the chicken and beef pieces. Make sure all pieces are coated with the marinade. Let them marinate for about 30 minutes in the refrigerator.

4 If you use wooden skewers, soak them in water for about 30 minutes so they won't burn.

5 Prepare the vegetables. Peel any vegetables that need the skins removed. Cut the zucchini into 1-inch (2.5-cm) pieces. Cut the onions into quarters.

6 Now create your kebabs. Choose some of the vegetables, one shrimp, and one cube each of chicken and beef. Stick the skewer through each piece of food. When your skewer is full, start on another skewer.

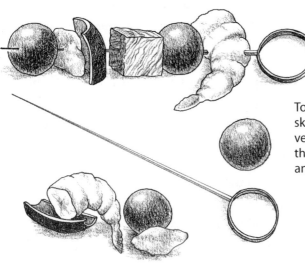

To make kebabs, stick skewers through the vegetables and the meat, chicken, and shrimp.

7 Prepare the rice, following the directions on the box.

8 Place the *kushiyaki* on the **broiling pan** (a shallow, open container used for broiling food) and brush any remaining marinade over all the food. *Ask an adult* to help you adjust the oven rack to the top third of the oven. Don't place the oven rack directly under the broiler's coils. Turn the oven to broil, let it heat up for a few minutes, then cook the kebabs about 10 minutes or until completely cooked, turning once during cooking. *Ask an adult* to help you turn the skewers. Or, you can grill your *kushiyaki*. *Ask an adult* to help you with the grill.

9 *Ask an adult* to remove the broiling pan from the oven. Place two skewers of *kushiyaki* on each plate. Use the fork to slide the pieces off the skewers, serve yourself and a friend some rice, and dig in. Be careful, the skewers are hot!

© 1999 Courtesy of Sunshine Grills, Inc.

Australian Barbecue

If you visit the land down under, you'll enjoy an Australian barbecue and eat grilled foods like beef steaks, **snags** (Australian sausages), lamb, pork, **prawns** (shellfish), **spuds** (potatoes) wrapped in foil, and lots of onions. The Australian barbecue grill, or barbie, as the Australians call it, usually has a solid, steel surface called a plate on one side and a grated surface on the other side. Many people grill on the barbie year-round.

Bratwurst

Historical records show that people in Greece were eating sausages as long ago as the ninth century B.C. These sausages were usually made from the intestines of animals, into which meat was stuffed. Today we eat many different kinds of sausages, from pork breakfast links to hot dogs to Italian sausages. Gourmet shops even sell chicken and apple sausages, and health food stores sell tofu (pronounced TOH-foo) sausages.

Spanish kids love a spicy sausage called chorizo (pronounced chor-EE-zoh) and enjoy eating this sausage sliced and fried with onions. If you visit New Orleans, La., you'll munch on a Cajun pork sausage made with lots of garlic called andouille (pronounced an-DOO-ee).

There are lots of different kinds of sausages, or wurst, in Germany, but the four main kinds are bratwurst (pronounced BRAHT-voorst), *kochwurst* (pronounced KOH'kh-voorst), *brühwurst* (BREW-voorst), and *rohwurst* (pronounced ROH-voorst). Beef sausages from the city of Frankfurt in Germany are called frankfurters, or dachshunds, which means "little dogs." One of the traditional ways to eat German sausages is with mustard and sauerkraut.

Here's What You Need

SERVINGS: 2

Ingredients

- [ ] nonstick cooking spray
- [ ] 2 bratwurst*
- [ ] sauerkraut (optional)
- [ ] 2 hot dog buns
- [ ] German mustard (optional)

*If you don't like bratwurst, you can use hot dogs.

Equipment

- [ ] frying pan or grill
- [ ] tongs

COOKING UP SOME HISTORY

When German immigrants brought the frankfurter to the United States, the hot dog was born.

So how did this little sausage go from frankfurter to hot dog? It happened because of a cartoon. In 1901, Harry Stevens had a food stand at the New York Polo Grounds and told his workers to yell, "Get dachshund sausages while they're red hot!" Tad Dorgan, a sports cartoonist at the polo match, needed to draw something for the paper, and when he heard what the workers were yelling, he quickly drew a cartoon of barking dachshund sausages, and called them hot dogs because he couldn't spell dachshund. After that, these little frankfurters became known as hot dogs.

Here's What You Do

1 Spray the frying pan with the cooking spray. (If you grill the bratwurst, *ask an adult* to help you.)

2 Heat the pan on medium heat for a few minutes. Place the bratwurst in the pan and cook until lightly browned, using the tongs to turn the bratwurst occasionally while cooking.

3 Remove the lightly browned bratwurst from the pan and keep them warm.

4 Heat the sauerkraut, following the directions on the bag or can.

5 Place the bratwurst in the buns, spread on some German mustard, and top with sauerkraut.

tasty tidbits

Check out some of these toppings for hot dogs:

New York City Dog Steamed onions and yellow mustard.

Chicago Dog Yellow mustard, dark green relish, chopped raw onions, tomato slices, celery salt, and a poppy seed bun.

Baltimore Frizzled Dog A deep-fried split hot dog.

Kansas City Dog Sauerkraut and melted Swiss cheese on a sesame seed bun.

Southern Slaw Dog Coleslaw.

Coney Island Dog Ground beef cooked with mustard, chili sauce, and onions, or sometimes just chili sauce and onions.

Bowwows

The hot dog became so popular in the early to mid-1900s in the United States that **diners** (roadside restaurants manufactured to look like railroad dining cars) started serving this food. Waitresses and cooks had their own language for food orders, called lunch counter slang. Lunch counter slang was a short, quick way for the waitress to give the food order to the cook. If you wanted a hot dog, the waitress called the order in as a bunpup, Coney Island, groundhog, or bowwow. People living in the United States today eat more than 20 billion hot dogs a year.

© 1999 Gary Braman

Stir-Fried Rice

-CHINA-

Rice is a very old grain. Historians believe that rice originated in South Asia and has been **cultivated** (grown) since about 5000 B.C. It is a staple in the diets of almost half the people of the world. There are well over 7,000 different varieties of rice. You can eat brown or white rice, or short-, medium-, or long-grain rice, jasmine rice, wild rice, **arborio** (pronounced ar-BOH-ree-oh) rice, a short-grain rice grown in Italy, and many more varieties.

COOKING UP SOME HISTORY

For centuries, the Ojibwa harvested wild rice in the waters of Lakes Michigan and Superior in eastern North America. This type of wild rice was a staple in their diet and played an important part in religious ceremonies. While the rice was being harvested from birch bark canoes, much of the grain fell back into the water, where new plants would grow the following year. With this method of harvesting, the Ojibwa knew there would be enough rice to feed their people each year.

Rice is an important part of daily meals in Asia. In Korea, *hin pap* (pronounced heen pop), which means white rice, is served at every meal, including breakfast. A favorite meal in Japan is sushi (pronounced SOO-shee), slices of fresh, raw fish, eaten with boiled rice that has been flavored with sweetened rice vinegar. Spanish kids love paella (pronounced pi-AY-yuh), a dish brimming with saffron rice, shellfish, chicken, pork, fish, peppers, onions, and chorizo, a spicy pork sausage. In Cameroon, in Africa, coconut rice with carrots, peppers, coconut milk, and onions makes a sweet meal.

Chinese fried rice comes from the Canton region in southeastern China and is cooked in a wok (pronounced wahk), which is a deep, round-bottomed pan. The best way to make this delicious meal is to **stir-fry** (cook food by quickly moving it around in a hot pan with very little oil) the ingredients separately and then mix them all together.

Here's What You Need

SERVINGS: 4
Recipe requires adult help.

Ingredients
- 1 small yellow onion
- 3 scallions
- 6 water chestnuts
- ½ cup (120 ml) frozen peas
- 2 cups (480 ml) cold, cooked white rice
- 2 eggs
- 1 tablespoon (15 ml) soy sauce
- 1 teaspoon (5 ml) sugar
- 2–3 tablespoons (30–45 ml) vegetable oil
- ½ teaspoon (2.5 ml) salt

Equipment
- knife
- cutting board
- 7 small bowls
- measuring cup
- whisk
- measuring spoons
- wok or large frying pan
- large spoon
- chopsticks (optional)

Here's What You Do

1 Peel the onion and chop it on the cutting board, and place it in one of the small bowls. Cut off the ends of the scallions and slice the scallions on an angle. Place these in the bowl with the onions.

Slice scallions on an angle.

2 Slice the water chestnuts into thin pieces. Place these in the second bowl. Place the peas in the third bowl and place the rice in the fourth bowl.

3 Crack the eggs into the fifth bowl and beat lightly with the whisk.

4 Mix the soy sauce and sugar together in the sixth bowl, whisk until blended, and set aside.

5 Heat the wok on high heat. The wok should be hot, but not smoking. If it starts to smoke, then turn the heat down to medium-high. *Ask an adult* to help you add 1 tablespoon (15 ml) of oil. Pour the eggs in the wok so the eggs coat the inside of the wok. When the eggs are almost cooked, break them up with the spoon into medium-sized pieces and stir-fry for a minute, then remove the pieces to the seventh bowl.

Pour the beaten eggs down the side of the wok so the eggs coat the inside of the wok.

6 Add another tablespoon (15 ml) of oil to the wok. Add the rice and stir-fry for a few minutes, then return the rice to its original bowl.

7 If the wok needs more oil, you can add the last tablespoon (15 ml). Add the onion and scallions to the wok and stir-fry for a few minutes. Then add the water chestnuts and peas and stir-fry for a few more minutes.

8 Add the soy sauce and sugar mixture to the wok and stir-fry for a minute.

9 Put the rice and eggs back in the wok and add the salt. Stir-fry for a few minutes until hot. *Ask an adult* to help you serve the fried rice. Don't forget to use chopsticks!

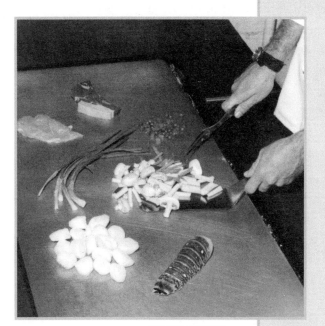

© 1999 Gary Braman

Culture Link

Mongolian Barbecue

To celebrate their hunting successes, the warriors of Kublai Khan, the Mongolian ruler of the Mongol or Yuan dynasty in China, which lasted from about A.D. 1279 to A.D. 1368, used their shields, heated by a fire, to quickly cook thin slices of meat and vegetables. That was the beginning of Mongolian barbecue. But you won't have to use a shield to cook your food if you visit a Mongolian barbecue restaurant. You can pick from a variety of fresh chopped vegetables, meats, seasonings, and rice, and let the chef stir-fry your meal while you watch.

Potjiekos

People in many cultures cook their main meals all in one pot, or **casserole** (a lidded pot used for slow, moist cooking in the oven or on top of the stove). Meals cooked in casseroles usually are cooked slowly for many hours. Almost any ingredient can be added to these meals, like meats, vegetables, grains, and pasta.

Visit Tunisia, a country in North Africa, and you will feast on lamb **tagine** (stew) with chestnuts, chickpeas, other vegetables, and spices. Kids in Ireland love Irish stew, a traditional meal made with layers of seasoned lamb, potatoes, and onions which is cooked slowly in water for 2 to 3 hours. Many Jews in Israel eat *dfina* (pronounced deh-FEE-nah) on the Sabbath. This stew, made with beans, potatoes, onions, beef, and spices, is slowly cooked overnight and eaten the following day.

In South Africa, *potjiekos* (pronounced poy-KEE-kohs) is a traditional dish. The word *potjiekos* means "food from one pot" and is from the Afrikaans language, which is spoken in South Africa by many people. Meat, spices, and a variety of vegetables, such as potatoes, sweet potatoes, green beans, and onions, are layered in a large black pot, which is covered and placed on an open fire outside to cook for many hours. When you make *potjiekos,* you can use the stove instead.

COOKING UP SOME HISTORY

The **Boers** (South Africans of Dutch or French descent), who settled in Cape Town, were among the first to make *potjiekos.* They made this dish on their long treks to settle in other areas in South Africa in the 1830s. They cooked this meal in large iron pots on open fires outdoors. This method of cooking is still used today. People enter cooking contests to see who can make the best *potjiekos* using the same methods as their ancestors.

Here's What You Need

SERVINGS: 6
Recipe requires adult help.

Ingredients

- 4 strips of bacon
- 1 medium yellow onion
- 1 clove of garlic
- 2 carrots
- handful of string beans
- 1 large potato
- 1 large sweet potato
- $2\frac{1}{2}$ pounds (1 kg) cubed, boneless beef chuck
- 1 teaspoon (5 ml) salt
- ground black pepper to taste
- 2 tablespoons (30 ml) flour
- 2 tablespoons (30 ml) oil
- spices (curry, turmeric, chili powder*)
- 3 teaspoons (15 ml) chopped parsley
- 20 ounces (600 ml) beef broth

Equipment

- cutting board
- sharp knife
- 5 medium-sized bowls
- vegetable peeler
- large bowl
- measuring spoons
- mixing spoon
- large, heavy casserole with lid
- measuring cup

*Don't use a lot of chili powder, as it makes foods very spicy.

Here's What You Do

1 Cut up the bacon and vegetables on the cutting board and set them aside until you need them.

  a. Cut the bacon into 2-inch (5-cm) pieces. Don't trim off the fat. Place the bacon pieces in the first bowl.

  b. Peel and chop the onions and place them in the second bowl.

  c. Peel the garlic and mince it into small pieces. Place it in the third bowl.

  d. Peel the carrots and slice them into thick pieces. Place them in the bowl with the garlic.

  e. Cut the ends off the string beans, then cut the beans in half. Place them in the fourth bowl.

  f. Peel the potatoes and cut them into thick slices. Place them in the fifth bowl.

2 Place the cubed beef chuck in the large bowl. Sprinkle the salt, pepper, and flour all over the meat. Use the mixing spoon to toss the meat in the bowl, coating all the pieces, and set aside.

3 Place the bacon in the casserole and turn the heat to medium. Once the bacon starts sizzling,

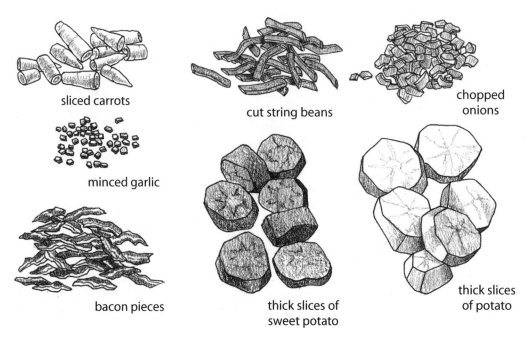

sliced carrots

minced garlic

cut string beans

chopped onions

bacon pieces

thick slices of sweet potato

thick slices of potato

cook it for about 5 minutes, stirring occasionally using the spoon. Then add the onions and sauté for a few more minutes until the onions are soft but not brown.

4 Place the garlic and carrots in the casserole and cook about 5 minutes, stirring occasionally. Remove all the food from the casserole and set it aside in one of the bowls.

5 Add the oil to the casserole and heat it on medium for a few minutes. Add the meat to the casserole and brown it on all sides about 5 to 10 minutes. Use the spoon to move the meat around occasionally as it cooks. Adjust the heat as needed so the meat browns. After the meat browns, take the casserole off the burner.

6 Now you will layer the food in the casserole. Leave all the meat at the bottom of the casserole, packed tightly together. *Lightly* sprinkle the spices and 1 teaspoon (15 ml) of the parsley over the meat. Place the cooked bacon and vegetables on top of the meat. *Lightly* sprinkle spices and another teaspoon (15 ml) of parsley over this layer. Place the string beans next, and the sliced potatoes on top. *Lightly* sprinkle spices and the last teaspoon (15 ml) of parsley on the top layer. *Do not stir.*

7 Add the beef broth around the outside of the layered food, cover the casserole, and simmer on low to medium-low heat for about 3 hours. Check once during cooking, about halfway through, to make sure there is enough liquid in the casserole and that the stew isn't boiling. Add some water if necessary. The food should cook at a low simmer the entire time. When the meal is completely cooked, stir once before serving.

 **tasty tidbits** There are a lot of different kinds of casseroles you can use to make a one-pot meal. Maybe you have one of these in which to cook your *potjiekos:*

Roaster A large metal cooker that is used in the oven.

Electric slow cooker A countertop cooker that will simmer your meal without the need for an oven or stove.

Clay baker An earthenware cooker that goes in the oven.

Dutch oven A cast-iron cooker that can go in the oven or on top of the stove.

© 1997 Malcolm O'Neill, New Zealand Nature Safaris

Culture Link

Hangi

The Maori (pronounced MOW-ree) are the original inhabitants of New Zealand. The Maori cook a meal called *hangi* (pronounced HUNG-ee), which means "earth oven," since this meal is cooked underground for 3 to 4 hours. After a pit is dug, a layer of wood and then stones are placed in the pit. The wood is lit and the pit heats up. When the stones are hot, a layer of leaves is placed on the stones, then the food goes on the leaves and is covered with a last layer of leaves. Before the pit is closed, water is thrown into the pit to create steam. Traditionally, foods like lamb, pork, fish, shellfish, sweet potatoes, and pumpkins are cooked and eaten at this feast. Maori are not the only ones who enjoy *hangi,* as shown here.

Macaroni and Cheese

-UNiTED STATES-

Cheese dates back to about 9000 B.C. Most food historians believe that the first cheese was made in the Middle East by accident. Nomads filled pouches made from animals' stomachs with milk for long journeys. Sometimes when they went to take a drink, instead of finding milk in the pouch, they found a watery liquid and solid, white lumps. The lumps were cheese. An enzyme in the lining of the animal's stomach called rennin combined with the milk, the hot sun, and the movement from the galloping horse to make the first cheese! Today people make hundreds of different kinds of cheeses.

Many cultures combine pasta and cheese to make a tasty main dish. In Italy, fettuccine Alfredo (pronounced feht-tuh-CHEE-nee ahl-FREY-doh) combines flat, narrow noodles with a **Parmesan** (hard, dry cheese made from skimmed or partially skimmed cow's milk) cream sauce to make a very rich dish. Kids in Hungary love a dish called *turos teszta* (pronounced TWO-rosh TEST-tah), made with wide, flat noodles cooked with cottage cheese, sour cream, onions, and bacon. People in the Caribbean make a macaroni cheese pie with cheddar cheese, corn, tomatoes, elbow macaroni, and a little cinnamon.

Americans put macaroni and cheese together for the first time in the 1800s. Macaroni and cheese made a simple, inexpensive, healthy meal. About 1936, these two foods began to be packaged and sold together. According to legend, a salesman who worked for Kraft Foods tied envelopes of his company's grated American cheese to boxes of macaroni and asked grocers to sell them together. The combination caught on and soon the company put packets of cheese and macaroni together in one box.

Cooking Up Some History

American colonists were making homemade cheese in the 1600s. They brought some cheese-making equipment from England so they could continue to enjoy this food. Eventually, the cheese made in the United States developed a character all its own and became known as "Yankee cheese" and later as

American cheese. In 1851, a dairy farmer named Jesse Williams started the first American cheese factory in Rome, N.Y. Soon, American cheese factories sprang up around the country. Today many people enjoy eating this smooth, semi-soft cheese in sandwiches, on hamburgers, or cooked with other foods.

Here's What You Need

SERVINGS: 8
Recipe requires adult help.

- 2 quarts (2 liters) water
- 1 teaspoon (5 ml) salt
- 8 ounces (225 g) macaroni
- 2 tablespoons (30 ml) butter
- 2 tablespoons (30 ml) flour
- 12 ounces (360 ml) evaporated milk
- 4 ounces (120 ml) water
- 1/4 pound (115 g) Velveeta cheese
- 1/2 pound (225 g) shredded or cubed cheddar cheese
- salt, pepper, and paprika to taste
- plain bread crumbs

Equipment

- 2-cup (480-ml) measuring cup
- large pot
- measuring spoons
- mixing spoon
- colander
- glass ovenproof bowl or pan
- medium-sized pot
- wire whisk
- knife
- cutting board

Here are some famous cheeses from around the world:

England Cheshire, Stilton, and cheddar.

France Brie, Camembert, and Roquefort.

Italy Mozzarella, Parmesan, and provolone.

Switzerland Gruyère, Emmental, and Appenzeller.

United States Colby, Monterey Jack, and brick.

Here's What You Do

1 Preheat the oven to 350°F (175°C). Pour the larger amount of water in the large pot, add the salt, and bring to a boil on high heat. Add the macaroni, turn the heat down to medium, and cook according to the directions on the box. Stir occasionally so the macaroni doesn't stick to the bottom of the pot.

2 Place the colander in the sink. When the macaroni is done, *ask an adult* to carry the pot to the sink to drain the macaroni using the colander. Put the macaroni in the ovenproof bowl.

3 Melt the butter in the medium-sized pot on medium heat. Add the flour and whisk until well blended. Then add the evaporated milk and the smaller amount of water and whisk until blended and smooth.

4 Slice the Velveeta into cubes. Add the cubes and the shredded or cubed cheddar to the pot with the milk and cook, stirring continuously, until the cheese is melted. Turn off the heat.

5 Add salt and pepper to taste. Mix well.

6 Pour the cheese sauce over the macaroni and mix well, then sprinkle on some paprika and bread crumbs. Bake for 15 minutes, then turn the oven to the broil setting and broil the macaroni and cheese for about 1 to 2 minutes and *no longer*. This will lightly brown the bread crumbs. Remove the macaroni and cheese from the oven.

© 1999 Gary Braman

Welsh Rabbit

Throughout the United Kingdom (England, Northern Ireland, Scotland, and Wales) people enjoy eating a dish called Welsh rabbit, or rarebit as it is also called. But rabbit meat is not a part of this dish. The main ingredient is cheese. Gloucester cheese is melted in a pot with milk and English mustard and then poured over slices of English bread that have been toasted. Some people like putting this dish under the broiler to lightly brown the cheese.

PART FIVE

For the Sweet Tooth

People have been eating sweets since the beginning of time. Prehistoric rock art in Spain and Africa shows men gathering honey. The ancient Babylonians used honey mixed with grain, such as millet, and spices to make honey cakes. But eating dessert as a separate course at the end of a meal didn't become popular until the nineteenth century. Before that, sweets were eaten with other courses.

The word *dessert* comes from the French word *desservir,* meaning "to clear the table." Desserts come in all shapes, sizes, colors, textures, and flavors. Kids in Tunisia love to munch on orange-flavored doughnuts dipped in honey. Denmark is famous for its **pastries** (dough in which food is baked), such as *spandauer* (pronounced spun-DOW-er), which is baked with plenty of butter, nuts, fruit fillings, and pastry cream. Sweet **borek** (pastry) filled with dates makes a tasty dessert for kids in Iraq. In the Caribbean, people enjoy *duckanoo,* a dessert originally from western Africa. This pudding is made with coconut, cornmeal, raisins, milk, cinnamon, and nutmeg and is boiled in packets of foil.

If you have a sweet tooth, you'll love these desserts from around the world.

Sweet Rice with Coconut Custard

-THAILAND-

Custards are desserts that are made with milk, eggs, and sugar, usually cooked in some type of cup or mold. Sometimes custard is eaten plain with a spoon, or it can be put in pastry or cooked with other foods, such as rice. Custard sauce, such as crème anglaise (pronounced krehm ahn-glayz), is served over cake, fruits, or other desserts in France. During the fifteenth century in Italy, people ate custard with millet, a cereal grain.

People all over the world love custard. These desserts can be fancy, such as the French custard crème brûlée (pronounced krehm broo-lay), which means "burnt cream." Just before serving, this custard is sprinkled with brown or granulated sugar and quickly broiled. The sugar topping becomes caramelized, which makes it hard and brittle. Custard also can be quite simple, like the Native American pumpkin custard. In Spain, kids love flan (pronounced flahn), a sweet custard that is coated with liquid caramel.

In England, custard is a key ingredient in trifle (pronounced TRI-fuhl), a sponge cake covered with jam and custard and topped with whipped cream.

A delicious custard dessert from Thailand is made with sweet, sticky rice. The rice is made first and put in the refrigerator to cool. Then the custard is made. The warm custard and the cold rice are served together, which creates an interesting sensation.

Here's What You Need

SERVINGS: 6

Recipe requires adult help.

Ingredients

- [ ] 2 cups (480 ml) sweet, sticky rice*
- [ ] 14 ounces (420 ml) coconut milk**
- [ ] 1/2 cup (120 ml) sugar
- [ ] 1/2 teaspoon (2.5 ml) salt
- [ ] 1 cup (240 ml) coconut milk
- [ ] 1/2 cup (120 ml) granulated sugar
- [ ] 1/4 cup (60 ml) brown sugar
- [ ] 2 eggs
- [ ] 1 teaspoon (5 ml) vanilla

Equipment

- [ ] bowl
- [ ] colander
- [ ] steamer or cheesecloth
- [ ] metal rack
- [ ] large stove-top casserole
- [ ] measuring cup
- [ ] measuring spoons
- [ ] mixing spoon
- [ ] blender
- [ ] glass baking dish, 8 × 8 inches (20 × 20 cm)
- [ ] shallow baking pan
- [ ] pointed knife

*You can find sweet, sticky rice at Asian food markets.

**Most supermarkets and Asian markets carry coconut milk, including low-fat versions.

Here's What You Do

1 Soak the rice in a bowl of water overnight. Drain off the water in the morning using the colander.

2 Steam the rice in the steamer for about 30 minutes. If you don't have a steamer, place the rice in a large piece of cheesecloth. Tie or twist the ends of the cheesecloth together to make a bag around the rice. Place the bag on the metal rack in the casserole, and put water in the bottom. Make sure the bag of rice is not in the water. Bring the water to a boil on high heat, then lower the heat to medium so the water simmers. Cover the casserole and steam the rice for 30 minutes. Check the water occasionally so it doesn't dry out. Add water if needed.

3 While the rice is steaming, pour the 14 ounces (420 ml) of coconut milk, ½ cup (120 ml) of sugar, and salt in the bowl. Mix until well blended. When the rice is done, *ask an adult* to help you remove the bag from the casserole since it is very hot. Add the rice to the coconut milk mixture. Stir and set aside. When the mixture is cool, cover it and place it in the refrigerator.

4 Preheat the oven to 325°F (160°C). To make the custard, pour the 1 cup (240 ml) of coconut milk, the sugars, eggs, and vanilla into the blender and mix until blended. Pour the custard mixture into the glass baking dish and set aside.

5 Fill about a third of the shallow baking pan with hot tap water, then place the baking dish with the custard into the baking pan.

6 Bake the custard about 40 to 45 minutes. The hot water in the baking pan will help the custard in the baking dish set, or get firm. Check the custard for doneness by inserting the blade of a pointed knife into the center of the custard. If the knife does not come out completely clean, it's okay as long as the custard looks firm. It will finish setting once it is out of the oven.

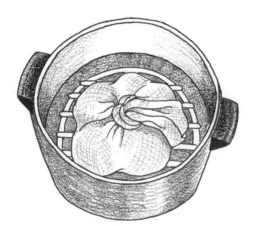

Place rice in cheesecloth, twist ends of cheesecloth together, and place bag on rack in deep stove-top cooker.

Cover stove-top cooker and steam rice.

7 When the custard is ready, serve a scoop of warm custard with some of the cold sweet rice.

© 1999 Gary Braman

Culture Link

Riz à l'Amande

The people in Denmark make a rice pudding that is eaten at the end of Christmas dinner. This pudding, called *riz à l'amande* (REE ah-lah-mahnd), combines the smooth texture of pudding with the crunchy texture of almonds and the light, fluffy texture of whipped cream, which is folded in to give this dessert an airy quality. *Riz à l'amande* is served with a spoonful of cold cherry sauce on top.

Baklawa

-EGYPT-

Many people like to end their meals with a sweet pastry. Some historians believe that the first pastries may have been made in ancient Greece. Bakers made little **tarts** (pastry crust with shallow sides, a filling, and no top crust) filled with grapes and almonds and wrapped them in fig leaves. Other historians believe that the ancient Egyptians were the first to make pastries with grain meal, honey, fruits, and spices.

Pastries come in all shapes and sizes. Puff pastries, puffy shells of baked dough, come with wonderful fillings like whipped cream and ice cream. Pastry for pie crusts is light and flaky. Phyllo (FEE-loh), which means "leaf" in Greek, is a tissue-thin dough that is used in layers to make the flakiest pastries.

Cooking Up Some History

Louis XIV, who ruled France from 1643 to 1715, had quite an appetite. It was not unusual for him to feast on eight-course meals, the last two courses consisting of pastries, fruits with sweet cream, sugared almonds, biscuits, and **marzipan** (a sweet mixture of ground almonds, sugar, and sometimes egg whites). Because of his sweet tooth, eating sweets with meals became a daily ritual. But eating all that food may have had a strange effect on the king. After his death, the autopsy results reportedly revealed that his intestines were twice the length of the average man's!

All cultures make unique and interesting pastries. Austrian kids love strudel, which consists of many thin layers of flaky dough with a fruit filling that are rolled up before baking. Cannoli (pronounced kan-OH-lee) is an Italian dessert consisting of a tube-shaped pastry shell that is filled with a sweet cream filling often mixed with bits of chocolate or nuts. In Algeria, gazelle's horns are pastries with a curved shape that are loaded with ground almonds and sprinkled with powdered sugar. In New Orleans, "little ears" are served with a praline (pronounced PRAY-leen) sauce made from brown sugar, pecans, and corn syrup.

Egyptian kids eat baklawa (pronounced BAHK-lah-wah) as a special treat. There are many different versions of baklawa eaten all over the Middle East. This version uses phyllo dough that is rolled into a log and then cut at an angle. In other countries, like Greece, the baklawa (spelled baklava) is made with layered phyllo dough and cut into diamond shapes.

Here's What You Need

Servings: 8

Ingredients

- [ ] 1 cup (240 ml) chopped nuts, any kind
- [ ] 1 cup (240 ml) flaked coconut
- [ ] 3 tablespoons (45 ml) softened butter
- [ ] 1 box phyllo*
- [ ] nonstick cooking spray, butter-flavored
- [ ] nonstick cooking spray (not butter-flavored)
- [ ] 1 cup (240 ml) sugar
- [ ] 1 cup (240 ml) water
- [ ] 1 teaspoon (5 ml) lemon juice
- [ ] ½ teaspoon (2.5 ml) vanilla sugar**
- [ ] 1 teaspoon (5 ml) butter

Equipment

- [ ] mixing spoon
- [ ] measuring cup
- [ ] medium-sized bowl
- [ ] wax paper
- [ ] paper towels
- [ ] cutting board
- [ ] sharp knife
- [ ] baking sheet
- [ ] small saucepan
- [ ] measuring spoons
- [ ] whisk
- [ ] wire rack
- [ ] shallow baking pan
- [ ] metal spatula

*Most supermarkets and all Middle Eastern markets sell phyllo. Make sure it is completely thawed before using.

**Vanilla sugar is a coarse sugar and can be found in Middle Eastern markets and gourmet food stores.

Here's What You Do

1 Preheat the oven to 300°F (150°C). Use the spoon to mix the chopped nuts and flaked coconut together in the bowl. Then add the softened butter and mix well.

2 Remove the phyllo from the box, carefully unroll the sheets, and lay them flat on your work surface. Phyllo dries out quickly, so place a sheet of wax paper over the phyllo and cover the wax paper with damp paper towels. Take 1 phyllo sheet and lay it on a large cutting board or other clean surface. Phyllo can tear easily when handled. The first few sheets will probably tear, so put them aside and use the first sheet that peels off without tearing.

3 Lightly spray the entire surface of the first phyllo sheet with the butter-flavored cooking spray. Lay 7 more sheets of phyllo on top of the first sheet, spraying each sheet with the butter-flavored cooking spray as you lay it down. Finally, spray the last, top sheet.

4 Spread the nut and coconut mixture in a line along one of the long edges of the phyllo. Lightly spray the mixture with the butter-flavored cooking spray. Starting at that edge, carefully roll the phyllo until you get to the other edge. It will look like a thick log. Lightly spray the log, especially the seam, with the butter-flavored cooking spray. Slice the phyllo log at an angle, dividing it into sections.

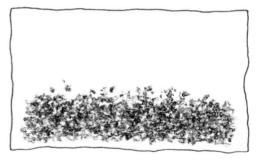

Spread nut and coconut mixture in long line along one long edge of phyllo sheets.

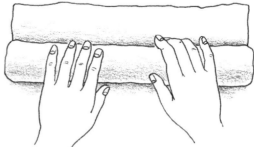

Roll phyllo until you get to other long edge.

Slice phyllo log at an angle.

5 Spray the baking sheet with cooking spray (do not use the butter-flavored variety for this). Place the pieces of baklawa on the baking sheet and bake for about 35 minutes or until lightly browned.

6 While the pieces are baking, make the "honey" syrup. Put the sugar, water, and lemon juice in the saucepan, whisk to blend, and bring to a boil at high heat, then turn down the heat to medium and simmer until the syrup thickens, about 20 minutes. Stir occasionally. Add the vanilla sugar and the butter and stir until the butter is melted. Turn off the heat and set the syrup aside.

7 Place the rack in the baking pan, then use the spatula to carefully place the pieces of baklawa on the rack to cool completely. Pour the honey syrup over all the pieces. Let the syrup drip off into the baking pan. Don't throw away the syrup that drips into the baking pan. Save it to drizzle over any leftover pieces of *baklawa* the next day.

© 1999 Gary Braman

Tropical Fruit Bowl

—SOUTH PACIFIC ISLANDS—

Many kids from around the world rarely eat sweets like cookies, cakes, pies, or pastries after their main meal. Instead, they enjoy eating fruit. And they never get bored because there are so many different fruits to choose from. Fruits from the South Pacific islands include pineapples, coconuts, papayas, kiwis, mangoes, and guavas.

Many kids in Europe eat fruit after their main meal. In France, cheese is often served with fruits such as grapes, pears, and raspberries. In Greece, figs are dipped in honey and yogurt. Sliced oranges sprinkled with cinnamon and dipped in a saffron yogurt make a tasty dessert in India.

In the South Pacific islands, tropical fruits such as papayas, mangoes, bananas, and pineapples are used in many desserts. In Tahiti, a yummy after-dinner treat is papayas baked in coconut milk. Another favorite way to serve tropical fruit is to cut up a bunch of different fruits, squeeze on a little lemon juice, sprinkle on some sugar, mix it up, and put it in bowls. Here's how to make your own South Pacific fruit bowl.

Here's What You Need

SERVINGS: 4
Recipe requires adult help.

Ingredients

- 2 kiwis
- 10 large strawberries
- 1 pineapple
- 1 orange
- 1 papaya
- 25 grapes
- flaked coconut

Equipment

- knife
- cutting board
- medium-sized bowl
- mixing spoon

Here's What You Do

1 Cut the skins off the kiwis. Cut the kiwis into slices and place them in the bowl. Rinse the strawberries, cut off the green tops, cut the berries into big pieces, and place them in the bowl with the kiwis.

2 *Ask an adult* to cut the pineapple in half lengthwise. Have the adult cut the fruit out of the shell. Cut the fruit into chunks and place them in the bowl. Save the pineapple shells to use as serving bowls.

Slice pineapple in half lengthwise.

Cut pineapple into chunks and put in bowl.

3 Peel the orange and then cut the fruit into chunks and place them in the bowl with the other fruits.

4 Cut the papaya in half and scoop out the seeds. Cut the halves into a few long slices, then peel off the skin. Cut the fruit into chunks and place them in the bowl.

5 Rinse the grapes and place them in the bowl. Use the spoon to mix the cut-up fruit together. Then divide the fruit between the two pineapple shells. Sprinkle on some flaked coconut. Though there are only two pineapple shells, this dish easily serves 4.

What's in a NAME?

You can thank the English for putting the word *straw* in *strawberries*. English farmers placed straw all around the plants to keep the berries off the damp soil.

Culture Link

Persian Melon

Long ago, the people who lived in what is now Iran were called Persians. They made many delicious meals and tasty desserts. A favorite dessert in modern Iran is Persian melon. Fruits like strawberries, grapes, peaches, and melons are cut up and served in scooped-out melon shells. This delicious dessert is served with a little mint and crushed ice.

© 1999
Gary Braman

Prairie Berry Cake

-CANADA-

Cakes have a long history. We know that ancient civilizations made honey cakes, such as the ones made by the Romans in the second century B.C. with barley grain and honey. The Romans also made a fruit cake with a mixture of grain, raisins, pine kernels, and pomegranate seeds. The ancient Egyptians invented the oven and baked many varieties of cakes.

Today cakes are still a favorite dessert and are eaten for birthdays, to celebrate holidays, or for any occasion. Cakes can be fancy, with decorations and flowers made from icing as on wedding cakes, or plain with no icing, like some pound cakes. Cakes can have a light, airy texture, like angel food cake, or be heavy and dense, like holiday fruitcake.

How did pound cake get its name? This cake, which is baked in the shape of a loaf, was traditionally made with 1 pound (454 g) each of flour, butter, and sugar. Eggs and a flavoring, such as vanilla or lemon, were also added. Pound cakes are still very rich, with lots of butter and sugar, so they usually don't have icing. And today you also can buy pound cakes that are low in fat.

Black Forest cake from Germany is a rich cake made with chocolate, cherries, and heavy cream. In Morocco, you can eat serpent cake. No, it's not made from snakes, but it is shaped like a snake and filled with sweet almond paste. *Sachertorte* (pronounced SAH-kuhr-tohrt-uh) is an extremely rich Austrian cake made with layers of chocolate and jam, then covered in a creamy chocolate glaze.

In Saskatchewan, a province of Canada, prairie berry cake is made from local berries called saskatoons. Saskatoons are native to Alberta, another province of Canada, and look a lot like blueberries. When ripe, they are almost black in color. The Plains Indians of Canada ate saskatoons fresh and dried them for use in other foods. European settlers used saskatoons in many of their recipes, a favorite being prairie berry cake. Now you can make your own prairie berry cake, but you can use blueberries if you can't find saskatoons.

Here's What You Need

SERVINGS: ONE 8-INCH (20-CM) CAKE
Recipe requires adult help.

Ingredients

- [ ] nonstick cooking spray
- [ ] $\frac{1}{2}$ cup (120 ml) softened butter
- [ ] $\frac{1}{2}$ cup (120 ml) sugar
- [ ] 2 eggs
- [ ] $1\frac{1}{3}$ cups (320 ml) unbleached white flour
- [ ] 1 tablespoon (15 ml) baking powder
- [ ] $\frac{1}{4}$ teaspoon (1 ml) salt
- [ ] $\frac{1}{2}$ teaspoon (2 ml) cinnamon
- [ ] $\frac{7}{8}$ cup (210 ml) milk
- [ ] $1\frac{1}{2}$ cups (375 ml) fresh saskatoons or blueberries
- [ ] 4 ounces (125 g) cream cheese at room temperature
- [ ] 2 tablespoons (30 ml) softened butter
- [ ] 1 teaspoon (5 ml) vanilla
- [ ] 4 tablespoons (60 ml) powdered sugar

Equipment

- [ ] square baking pan, 8 × 8 inches (20.5 × 20.5 cm)
- [ ] electric mixer
- [ ] measuring cup
- [ ] medium-sized bowl
- [ ] measuring spoons
- [ ] rubber spatula

Here's What You Do

1 Preheat the oven to 350°F (175°C). Spray the baking pan with nonstick spray and set aside.

2 Use the electric mixer to beat the butter and sugar together. Then beat in the eggs.

3 In the bowl, combine the flour, baking powder, salt, and cinnamon.

4 Add about one-half of the flour mixture to the butter mixture and mix. Then add half the milk and mix, the rest of the flour and mix, and finally the rest of the milk and mix well for a minute or so.

5 Use the rubber spatula to fold in the saskatoons or blueberries. **Folding** means gently combining two or more ingredients. It involves using a down, across the bottom, up, and over motion to turn the ingredients over each other. Wash the spatula since you will use it later.

Fold berries into batter with spatula, using a down, across the bottom, up, and over motion.

6 Pour the batter into the baking pan and bake in the oven about 40 to 45 minutes, or until the cake is lightly browned and springs back when pressed lightly in the center. Let the cake cool completely before icing.

7 To make the icing, combine the cream cheese, softened butter, vanilla, and powdered sugar and beat with the electric mixer until fluffy. Use the spatula to spread the icing on the cake. Enjoy!

© 1999 Gary Braman

Culture Link

Äppelkaka

People in Sweden also make cakes with fruit. Swedish apple cake, *äppelkaka* (pronounced EHP-pel KAW-ka), is a delicious cake made with **poached** (cooked gently in water) apple halves that are layered in the bottom of a cake dish and topped with a rich batter made from ground almonds, butter, and eggs. This cake is usually made in autumn.

Nutmeg Cookies

—NORWAY—

Kids all over the world love cookies. Cookies make a great snack, a terrific dessert, and always find their way into lunch boxes. The word *cookie* is from the Dutch word *koekje* (pronounced CUCK-yuh), which means "little cake." Food historians believe it was not the Dutch who first made this tasty treat, but the seventh-century Persians, who were one of the first to cultivate sugar.

There are six basic types of cookies. Drop cookies are dropped by the spoonful onto a baking sheet before baking. Bar cookies are cut into bars after baking. Molded cookies are shaped with the hands. Pressed cookies are made using a cookie press. Refrigerator cookies are rolled into a log, kept cold, then sliced and baked. And rolled cookies are rolled out flat and cut with cookie cutters. Just about every culture makes some type of cookie, but it is not always called a "cookie."

What's in a NAME?

Here are some other names for cookies:

England Biscuits.
Spain *Galletas* (pronounced gah-YEAH-tahs).
Italy *Biscotti* (pronounced bee-SKOT-tee).
Germany *Keks* (pronounced kayks).

Christmas is a fun time in Germany because everyone gets to eat *Springerle* (pronounced SPRING-uhr-lee). When a carved wooden rolling pin is rolled over the dough, it leaves a beautiful design on the cookie. Chocolate chip cookies have been a favorite in the United States since the mid-1900s. Welsh cakes, sweet biscuit-like cookies made in Wales, part of the United Kingdom, include sugar, nutmeg, and **currants** (fruit that resembles raisins) and are cooked on a griddle.

Nutmeg cookies are a special treat for kids in Norway. Kids love to help by rolling out the dough and using cookie cutter shapes. These cookies are usually made for holidays like Christmas and Easter, but you don't have to wait for a holiday to make them.

Here's What You Need

SERVINGS: ABOUT 3 DOZEN COOKIES

Ingredients
- [ ] nonstick cooking spray
- [ ] $1/4$ pound (115 g) butter, softened
- [ ] $1/2$ cup (120 ml) powdered sugar
- [ ] 2 eggs
- [ ] $1/2$ tablespoon (7.5 ml) milk
- [ ] $1/2$ teaspoon (2.5 ml) nutmeg
- [ ] $1/4$ teaspoon (1 ml) lemon juice
- [ ] 2 cups (480 ml) flour
- [ ] 1 teaspoon (5 ml) baking powder
- [ ] granulated sugar, small amount

Equipment
- [ ] baking sheet
- [ ] measuring cup
- [ ] electric mixer
- [ ] small bowl
- [ ] wire whisk
- [ ] measuring spoons
- [ ] medium-sized bowl
- [ ] rolling pin
- [ ] cookie cutters in various shapes
- [ ] rubber spatula
- [ ] pastry brush
- [ ] metal spatula
- [ ] wire rack

Cooking Up Some History

Chocolate chip cookies are the most popular cookie in the United States, thanks to Ruth Wakefield, the woman who created them. In 1930, she and her husband bought an old toll house in Massachusetts and opened it as a lodge, calling it the Toll House Inn. One day Ruth broke off pieces from a Nestlé semisweet chocolate bar and added them to her cookie dough. She baked the cookies and was surprised to find the chocolate pieces did not melt completely. Her recipe was a big hit. The Nestlé company found out about her recipe and made her a deal. Nestlé got the rights to print her recipe on wrappers of Nestlé chocolate bars in exchange for all the chocolate she could use for the rest of her life. Later, Nestlé began selling bags of chocolate chips, where you'll still find Ruth's recipe.

Here's What You Do

1 Preheat the oven to 350°F (175°C). Lightly spray the baking sheet with cooking spray and set aside.

2 **Cream** (mix until smooth and creamy) the butter and sugar together in the mixer.

3 Beat *one* of the eggs in the small bowl with the wire whisk. Add the egg, milk, nutmeg, and lemon juice to the mixer and mix well.

4 In the medium-sized bowl, mix the flour and baking powder together. Add the flour and baking powder mixture to the mixer and mix well until it forms into dough.

5 Using the rolling pin, roll the dough out on a clean flat surface to about ¼ inch (0.5 cm) thick. Cut out the

Roll dough to about ¼ inch (0.5 cm) thick.

cookies with the cookie cutters, then use the spatula to lift the cookies off the work surface and onto the baking sheet.

Cut out cookies with cookie cutters.

6 Beat the second egg in the small bowl. Brush a little of the beaten egg on the top of each cookie, then sprinkle each cookie with a little sugar.

7 Bake the cookies for about 10 minutes. Use the metal spatula to remove the cookies to the wire rack. Let cool on the wire rack.

Culture Link

Figolla

© 1999 Gary Braman

There is a small island in the Mediterranean Sea just south of Sicily called Malta. Kids in Malta eat a traditional biscuit-like cookie called a *figolla* (pronounced FEE-gohl-ah). After the dough is mixed and rolled out, kids use large cookie cutter shapes of animals, baskets, and people, cutting out two of every shape. Then they sandwich marzipan filling in between the two shapes. The edges are sealed and the shapes are baked and decorated with icing to make a deliciously sweet cookie for Easter.

Glossary

adobe   A sun-dried brick made of clay and straw.

arborio   A short-grain rice grown in Italy.

Berbers   Aboriginal peoples of North Africa who make up a large part of the populations of Libya, Algeria, and Morocco. Most make a living as farmers, but some are nomadic.

Boers   South Africans of Dutch or French descent.

borek   Iraqi pastry.

broil   To cook directly above or below a heat source.

broiling pan   A shallow, open container used for broiling food.

cacao   A tropical tree that produces a seed used to make chocolate, cocoa, and cocoa butter.

casserole   A lidded pot used for slow, moist cooking in the oven or on top of the stove.

cream   To mix until smooth and creamy.

crumpets   Small, flat, muffin-like cakes.

cultivate   To grow.

currant   A fruit that resembles a raisin.

custard   A pudding-like food made with milk and eggs.

dim sum   A variety of dishes including steamed or fried dumplings, shrimp balls, steamed buns, and Chinese pastries.

diners   Roadside restaurants manufactured to look like railroad dining cars.

fold   To gently combine two or more ingredients. A down, across the bottom, up, and over motion is used to turn the ingredients over each other.

Franklin Institute   An organization named for Benjamin Franklin that fosters the development of science and technology.

griddle   A flat pan used for frying.

knead   To squeeze, press, or roll dough with the hands.

marinade A seasoned liquid in which foods like meat, fish, and vegetables are soaked to absorb the flavor of the liquid.

marinate To soak.

marzipan A sweet mixture of ground almonds, sugar, and sometimes egg whites.

Middle Ages A period in history from about A.D. 500 to A.D. 1500.

mince To cut into very small pieces.

mineral water Water from underground springs that has minerals and bubbles from carbon dioxide.

miso A soybean paste used in soups.

nomads Wanderers with no permanent home.

Olmecs An ancient Central American civilization.

Parmesan A hard, dry cheese made from skimmed or partially skimmed cow's milk.

pastry Dough in which food is baked.

plantain A tropical fruit similar to a banana.

poach To cook gently in water.

prawn Shellfish.

purée To blend to a thick consistency.

saffron A yellow spice used to flavor and color food.

samovar A metal container with a spigot used to boil water for tea.

satay Small cubes of meat placed on skewers and grilled or broiled.

sauté To fry lightly in fat.

skewer Pointed sticks used for cooking.

snag Australian sausage.

spud Potato.

staple A main food source.

steep To soak in liquid.

stir-fry To cook food by quickly moving it around in a hot pan with very little oil.

tagine Tunisian stew.

tart A pastry crust with shallow sides, a filling, and no top crust.

Vikings Norwegian explorers who lived from A.D. 700 to A.D. 1000.

whisk To stir using a fast, circular motion.

yeast A one-celled fungus.

Index

Recipe entries have initial capital letters